the
new york
diary

ALSO BY NED ROREM

The Paris Diary of Ned Rorem
Music from Inside Out

the
new york
diary
of
ned rorem

GEORGE BRAZILLER

New York

contents

PART 1
Aboard the 'S.S. United States'
October 1955

*If you look back, you risk turning
into a statue of salt—that is, a statue of
tears. . . .*

—COCTEAU

It's not that I'm more self-involved than other people, I'm just more free about showing it. Exhibitionist: that has the ring of a dirty word. Yet an artist is an exhibitionist by definition, and an artist cannot be dirty.

Now shyness forces me, all seasick, back to this journal. Hopefully it will be at once less frivolous and more outspoken than those Paris diaries. One grows increasingly unconcerned about others' eccentricities if they begin to displace one's own.

Where am I? The man-as-artist can begin again only in midstream, that place where there's time for time, where the future can't loom, the past sheds its skin, and where we finally find ourselves *in the fact.*

▼▼▼

Yesterday was my birthday. Tomorrow we arrive in New York. Neither event particularly thrills me this time although both involve years and years. All appears already to have happened to another little boy though I can still clearly see him running about. Will taxis *never* learn where we live? Must we tell them every time?

My Paris weathers have grown into a tremendous conglomeration so it's somewhat of a blur; later we are more clearly nostalgic about places least frequented since we have only *one* memory of them. It is no accident: a new explosion of events on the eves of leaving. I've too many recollections of the Gare d'Orsay for a general sentiment to remain hovering, but to these was added a

particular tussle at the *commissariat* on the eve of my going—
and Paris was quit with a bad taste. Not to mention an array of
old photographs Denise Bourdet showed me of today's dead and
dying in their beautiful time. Well really I can't tell what's
waiting for me "back home" (as travelers say) when the psychoanalytic examples (now, to me, long forgotten) come flying
through town more messy than ever in monster egoism.

Come snow, clean us off a little! The mediocrity of this ship's
passengers is beyond belief. But the mediocrity of this ship's pen
impedes me from developing more *là-dessus*. How could any
psychoanalysis help but be lugubrious now? Life's too long and
there seems nothing I cannot understand. Though sometimes I
pretend ignorance just to make time go by.

▼▼▼

The French speak for exercise, Americans for self-expression.
Paradoxically the French speak on many levels but Americans
on only one. Americans say what they think, the French think
what they say. As for me, I take everything I hear literally, and
mean literally nothing I say. And still hide all knives before
going out, not knowing whom I might bring home who'd stab
me.

▼▼▼

America is not a place one speaks about except in retrospect,
so the next months may be silent—that is, too noisy to think.

Yet to think—even to talk—about your life is, in a way, to
stop living, so a diary becomes a breathing corpse which eats into
the present. Possibly, writing music is also a kind of self-denial
(as well as self-indulgence), but no one can assert that it's
autobiographical. Music and prose satsify two distinct drives in
me, though each involves anesthetizing life temporarily to bring
order from chaos. But the music is sacred chaos while the prose
is ordered profanity. Being today involved in the latter (and time
stops in midocean) I halt to pluck green memories and mount

them in this scrapbook like drying fall leaves, leaves whose veins still flow with an inextricable poison that pervades and blurs the very system that formed them. . . . But I *do* have to live, don't I? No, I'll leave that to others. I just have to get my work done.

▼▼▼

Et pourtant . . . Recurring obsessions. The anguish of alcohol's danger, however imaginary or exaggerated, pains me still, and will doubtless continue until death, as will legends of Eros and fright of people and boredom and guilt about work. Still, we continue to live in order to be loved and maybe to love. There's little else.

▼▼▼

Adolescence is the only period when being-in-love is a potent force, for that's when the heart first breaks, breaks out of the placenta into our poignant confusion and reaches a quick peak. The average mind is adolescent. Therefore the run-of-the-mill have a truer capacity for love than intellectuals, who should know better.

▼▼▼

The hoped-for never materializes. Still, one cannot be positive of exactly knowing when the End's around—and who can say whether doubt might not be the ultimate joy?

▼▼▼

In art spontaneity must always be calculated. Simplicity is complex, to be easy is hard. Why do I compose? It keeps me off the streets. (At this moment I could say: keeps me out of the waves.)

We live mostly in the past or future. Music and meals and sometimes mating are all that exist in the present.

There goes the dinner gong. Despite seasickness I shall reel down and eat. Because I've paid for it.

▼▼▼

Then, to make time go by until we land (pretending ignorance), and because America is not a diary country (its inhabitants preferring to make others live their thoughts) let me look back to reactions of those three months three years ago when I first returned there. At the Chelsea Hotel, autumn of 1952.

New Yorkers, the New Yorkers who were my friends, had made a shroud for the city during that period of the Eisenhower election. I saw this both half and twice as well because I had never thought about it and still was a stranger come home. The delirium of old acquaintance past, and I nearly saw New York as a new Frenchman, had forgotten its former power over me as amply as that of an old love affair. And what if this were to happen as I went back into France? When and for how long would I be able to stay there once more before the arrival of death, which I now believed and feared and knew the secrets of? If I am special, then I can love only a daily person, but for this, or even for its memory, I would move to China. Should it be the opposite? No, as then there would no longer be love for me: the man not born a genius may know family joys but not those of travel; he must wait. The famous will displace themselves for the unknown. Or so I felt in '52.

It had been about four years. I read death on old friends' faces suddenly as an overnight change. Home in Philadelphia I thumbed through forgotten scores, heard old records, spent hours with baby pictures and high school annuals; nothing that was real had dimmed, rather had become surrealistically clear. I recalled each scratch on the family furniture, every piece of silverware, all curtains and smells and bedspreads, the same, the same only smaller, like photographs in dreams, or like being on a train taking my youth farther away. It was more than I could stand, even when I turned to look the other way. And oh, the anxiety of parents when they know together how far off this all has grown since they saw the first nasty glimmers of love and talent that kidnapped their child. . . .

Although I drank, I did not make love in New York. (Do I write this in hope that love may arrive tonight, even as I write of atomic fright feeling that written words prevent the reality?) Although I had again fallen down there and seen a thousand former friends, not making love made me miss insanely my Paris. The streets were full of the globe's cleanest sunshine, but Americans seemed afraid of love, still talked psychotherapy as though I'd never gone away. All about me on Park Avenue in the bright of noon I saw people, young people, vomiting, bleeding, lying on their backs with vacant stares, begging, limping, having epileptic fits; old friends were dead, disappeared, in asylums, or forgotten in medical wards; these street-sleepers were invisible to my friends who live there, but I saw panic at any corner turned and not a trace of the marvelous indifference that the Latin church affords. Even their music had hysteria, and what didn't exist in France existed too much at home.

There was no place I had not been, nothing I had not done or seen, nobody not known and loved; yet all of it wrong. For I had not been able to observe the cinema of myself. Why do I keep on, making every gesture in the fear and hope that it will be seen, remembered? Or for what reason can I say that this or that of me I have made indelible, when with a final gulp I, too, have admitted death? And when I die people may talk a little while, ten, fifteen years, saying, "Remember when he did such and such a thing," or, "It's tragic that with such a talent and etc. . . ." Then those who've said it will also die, and fifty years after, it will be as if none of us had ever . . . etc.

A printed song is no longer *me*. I hold out my arms for a bit, but it gets away, and I must start again. When it is sung in concerts I cringe that a half-recollected infant of mine may disgrace himself. If ever I am spoken of in whatever generations may have the funny miracle of being born, it will not be Ned Rorem *himself* who is remembered. I loathe this thought.

▼▼▼

I went alone one evening to the Chaplin movie *Limelight*. (Like all great comics, Chaplin lacks a sense of humor.) Afterwards dined alone in the 23rd Street automat (an old beef pie, spastics, ladies with runny noses, people who don't say "Excuse me!"). Then returned to the hotel room alone feeling like Tobias Mindernicle. Nothing to do but finish the book I'm reading, take one of my rare baths, go to bed: terrible remedies for a big city. France had saved my life four years before and would do so again. But the weather had been heavenly since my return and I felt neither sad nor happy. I'd seen so many people good and bad in so short a time that I had no moment for ideas.

▼▼▼

Alma Morgenthau asked me that autumn if being goodlooking had caused difficulties professionally. Others had wondered this, and what is the answer? I began writing music at birth, before knowing what composers were supposed to look like. The surnormality of "creation" hit me before I was aware that problems divorced from art show up for any adolescent. Nobody knows where talent comes from, whether it's cause or effect, but it seems clearly not inherited since it grows so rarely and in such diversified climates, and usually becomes apparent before worldly stimulants could direct it for better or for worse. I would have been a composer no matter how I looked; had I been born deformed I simply would have made another kind of music.

Appearance has never fundamentally helped me. Those who have been most useful are people I've never met. Artists are artists because of, and despite, their environment. If his father is great, no son will equal him, so that son must choose either another profession or suicide.

Intelligent beauty (a contradiction in terms) moves over an earth that never asked for beauty. Therefore beauty is shy. Not to have the problem of an awful face is to create different problems, different faces. We know what's great mostly by hearsay, by what surrounds us in the streets. I'm not sure that the first reading of an unknown Shakespeare would suddenly call forth his famous power. Beauty's not instantaneous (necessarily). Once the thing is done, dragged up by pain from nowhere, it seems simple. "I could have done it," they say. Yes, but did they? "My child, my cat, could have made that line, this noise." But they didn't.

Staring into the Chelsea bathroom mirror, I placed those scissors in my nose, a prong in each nostril, then opened them quickly—and zlish! blood everywhere! The pain dissolved into ice as I observed a diffuse orange glow like a halo around my skull. . . . Then I fainted. I was going back to France.

▼▼▼

"I'll love you forever" may be said by one person to many others with equal honesty. Time in love and time in life are unrelated: forever exists more than once. Where is P.? Alive. But no longer in the time of forever. Expose yourself to hurt, to love, or why live? Do we then have to live? Is working living? No.

▼▼▼

Of course the America of 1955 will be different. No, nothing again will ever be new, though every return necessarily indicates a change. At least I felt this on arriving, and said, "Here is the last marvelous displacement I will ever know: the bitter sweetness of a first homecoming." It's not true. The same voyage will always be new, and we all have perhaps but a few moments more. People, that's not memory. Sentiment is a situation recollected, the fainting taste of skin-covered blood. Greenwich Village, they say, is revitalized, though upper Broadway has always represented a land of the dead. But do we ever change? No.

Yes. Life doesn't stop. I feel myself involuntarily flung forward into 1955, even as I wish in this book to rush back toward unforgotten formations as though they made a difference. How I wish that Ned the grown-up could stand back aloof and cast a jaundiced eye at Ned the growing brat, conceited and insecure, could watch him misbehave and suffer while knowing full well that when he becomes the Ned of today he'll still suffer and misbehave as before.

▼▼▼

If there *is* always tomorrow, the tentative appeal or hope-giving element lies in the utterly unknown. The past, any past or present may form in a palm's lines, but never the future. That future, said to be divined by the extrasensorily perceptive (a mother's warning of her son's death overseas), is only an intensification of the present stated in terms of the past. Nobody knows the future. Cassandra saw only the illogical logic of human nature.

▼▼▼

Three weeks ago in London I bought a giant tube of K–Y. It is still unopened.

Who knows what New York may bring? Nell Tangeman will sublet her far-west 23rd Street apartment to me during the winter. But first I'll visit the family for a week in Philadelphia. Neither place can I yet perceive tonight because there's snow all over the ocean.

PART 2

New York

Spring 1956

One lives by memory . . . and not
by truth.

—STRAVINSKY

Ages since I've written here because, as prophesied, New York with its noisy pollution is where, unlike Paris, we look at our feet instead of the sky. No "inner repose" needed for journal writing. I'm not sure this is true. *Is* it repose French diarists possess?

In any case, Americans are not especially concerned about whether they're going to hell when they die, and that's the theme of a French diary. I'm not at all interested in what I now write here after such long months, and cannot imagine adding anything not already said at more urgent minutes. It's not simple to summon sufficient interest for starting again. We all lie anyway at the really fascinating time that makes a difference. When a person has gone to pieces—really to pieces—he is no longer capable of maintaining a document about himself although this is the crucially interesting moment toward which he has been directed, because he's no longer in a position of caring. Not that I've gone interestingly to pieces, *au contraire. La preuve,* I'm writing a diary once more.

▼▼▼

America, the new slang: goof—to miss, make a mistake. Flip—to swoon with enthusiasm. America, the new compulsion: male impersonation. In his *mépris* of women a young man refuses to caricature them; he becomes instead a male impersonator by affecting leather and dungarees (male symbols, it seems). He attends S. & M. meetings (i.e., sado-masochist or slave-master) where truly gory doings are rumored. Yet, when I question Bill

13

Flanagan about the details, the Third Avenue bartender, over-
hearing, intrudes: "Don't kid yourself—they just hit each other
with a lot of wet Kleenex!" Perhaps it's in mimicry of divine
James Dean (already immortalized by our Frank O'Hara); still,
it's a cause and not an effect: James Dean would not have
existed without them.

America, my "success"—otherwise I'd have been a failure. I
learned that a composer, whatever his reputation, must be (as
opposed to a poet) on the spot. I also touched Talullah Bank-
head (thanks to Bobby Lewis) and dined with Dietrich (thanks
to Truman Capote). Neither of these ladies knows I exist. *Et
puis après*. Talullah rose from her couch and exclaimed: "I'm not
so old yet that I can't stand up for a young man that wants to
meet me." As I was speechless, even *her* conversation lagged,
and that was that. [I shall meet her again in 1964 when I
compose music for an as-yet-unwritten drama by Tennessee
Williams in which Talullah will star for four fatal perform-
ances.]

As for Marlene, there we sat in El Morocco at midnight, she
all in black, with Harold Arlen, downing a four-course meal
including an oozing *baba au rhum,* and Truman's three other
guests pretending she was just someone else, and she so bored,
while I longed to lean over and whisper, "Oh, Miss Dietrich, I
loved you in this, and even more in that, and especially in *Song
of Songs,* which nobody knows," but lost my nerve and stayed
mute, and she never looked my way, but remained thin despite
the *baba,* hummed along with the solicitous pianist playing "Lili
Marlene," called over the *chasseur* ("How do you say *chasseur*
in English?"), to whom she gave a phone number and said,
"Tell them I can't come," without explaining who she was. Even
grander was the leave-taking: when Arlen gave her a handful of
change for the powder room she complained, "Oh no, darling, I
need a bill. After all, coming from me, *noblesse oblige!*"

I prefer to recall my enthusiasm of 1944 when, drunk at 5 A.M.,

I would phone from veneration to Povla Frijsh, then hang up when she answered. Today, knowing her, I am disenchanted. Or knowing George Copeland or other idols of my babyhood. More and more, despite myself, I am impervious to those about me and wander through daylight past all reactions like a somnambulist, aware only of me, or vaguely of the family unit, which takes new meaning. Before the age of thirty we can't know this, being charged with only accusation. There's no longer the desire for gossip to interest others. What's a diary? Write about the rain.

I made discoveries in New York and know it as one can only in getting away. Write about drinking in America: *je m'y connais un peu, quand même!* The best thing for a hangover (next to not drinking)—and this I hadn't known before—is that Manhattan array of rhapsodic turkish baths which answer so well to your one-track carnal awareness the afternoon after. Days, days can be spent there in the sensual naked steam of anonymity disintoxicating the body (always the body), while outside it ceaselessly rains, glumly rains to your total disinterest. It was my discovery of America and must be shown to all Latin visitors as an Anglo-Saxon attitude.

▼▼▼

Nothing exists unless it is notated, not even the smell of wind, much less the sound of pastorales. I remember sounds with the eye. Even love and lovemaking are unreal except through a recollection which grows faint and disappears unless I print it here. I can't "just live," but must be aware of being aware.

"Why do we live, since we must die?" everyone wonders, whereas the converse could as logically be asked. Maybe life is death and death life—like Pascal's sleep and waking. My sleep is so light, so light, just Miltown at night gets me through it. Quite simply, the purpose of life is to seek life's purpose; to find the right answer is not so important as the right question. Where we came from, where we'll go, and above all, why, we'll never never understand.

Can you polish a phrase about tears in your eyes with tears in
your eyes? Yes.

Who am I to say that Delius stinks? Every nonmusical
association from my sexy adolescence shrieks of him. Wagner too
I love, if I don't have to listen to him. For nothing *works* today.
Things must work: love, music. Or if they flop, they should flop
tragically, not tackily.

Title: *The Rewards of Boredom,* i.e., of sobriety. No one
believes it, but I'm much more timid than these journals indicate. Yet the fact of their existence proves it. If I utter brasheries
when dead sober it's to prove I *can* dead sober. I'm no longer
"mean" when drunk, just weepy and redundant. But my bite is
louder than my bark.

▼▼▼

Some of my best friends are 12-tone composers. David laughs
for Absalom. Fugue is as suspect as its opposite, improvisation.
(This applies to present decades.) Opera should be seen and not
heard—needs letter scenes, toasts, instruments on stage, candles,
dream sequences, and women dressed as men. (Men dressed as
women, however, can never be taken "seriously," i.e., as people
in love.) The bad old days. Two nuns take leave of each other
saying: Be good! Stravinsky–Cocteau *Oedipus*: a telegram from
Sophocles. I deserved the Gershwin Memorial Award (1949),
but the piece I wrote did not.

▼▼▼

Now I've known so many that'll die soon: Carl Van Vechten.
Who? Peter Watson and Cecil Smith. Honegger's dead too, and
now little Bernard Charpentier—*de la drogue.* Myself from
champagne, that easy way away from tension. Aphrodisiacs used
to be put, for children, into candy which is dandy though
liquor's quicker. . . . We do not need graphic sexuality in
letters. Nineteenth-century restraint's more troubling than to-

day's one-dimensional violence. . . . Taffy-colored taffeta drag: old-fashioned.

▼▼▼

Seven years' absence. Old friends in America are now settled into their mold. I am left out. Conservatism comes with age.

▼▼▼

The long lazy heat of childhood summers in the first heavy odor of zinnias, hollyhocks, bumblebees, summer with his hot yellow smile at the summer maid who sniffs the dirty laundry of the boy she loves.

▼▼▼

All we need now is one genius, just one. There aren't any more. I'm not as glamorous as my friends think. But more than they think, blind to the rich man who, in his huge and un-requited love, finances the lover of his sweetheart. The French have no word for vicarious.

▼▼▼

Embarrassment composing at the piano when Messaoüd was in the house. Messaoüd, our Moroccan servant in Fez, 1949, in every sense a Moslem and centuries away. Embarrassment that he might find the sounds I struck too corny.

Embarrassment as a child at the semi-annual arrival of the decorators who pulled away the bed to expose the lower wall onto which for six months I had smeared deposits of mucus after picking my nose in the morning.

▼▼▼

Sober: the awe of death is—is *sharper*. But sorrow is useless.

Drinking, like anti-Semitism, is unintelligent. But must we always be intelligent? Probably.

If through skill in false premises I annihilate a less logical yet more honest adversary, I later cringe with wonder at the pleasure in my wrongness. To be confusedly right (though ephemeral and smug) should be higher satisfaction, should it not? Does my conscience tell me *not* to kill because my wish tells me to kill?

If I've learned one thing in my travels it's that Europeans, Arabs, Negroes are not "just like everyone else" but quite different. That difference should be coveted, not thwarted, for it provides an attraction which could prevent rather than cause wars.

In war the first thing to go is the truth.

▼▼▼

People are mostly alike; one hopes for a difference. When a crippled girl entered the restaurant tonight I mused that there at least, by definition, was a difference. But then she brought forth *The Readers' Digest*.

▼▼▼

Discontent with work, vaguely but regularly saddened by the gorgeous weather—sentiments not wholly lacking in charm. Meanwhile the weeks slide by like a funeral procession.

▼▼▼

Another day . . .

▼▼▼

The superfluous is all that counts—art, screwing, ice cream. As for sleep or taxes, they don't *count*, do they?

▼▼▼

Painter friends accuse me of blindness. It is because I'm internally visual. Even my musical memory is visual, not auditory. For instance, if I'm on a subway or somewhere and think of a tune, I inscribe that tune on a mental staff, photograph it, store the negative elsewhere in my brain for development later.

Nor can I "just listen" anymore: whatever enters my mind must be inscribed on psychic paper. Do I *know* music too well now to enjoy it? In any event the layman's hearing is inconceivable to me; my nature always asks what makes beauty beautiful.

And silence? Becomes the sound of our world whirling through space.

▼▼▼

A poet may look like a janitor, a janitor like a poet. Art is the only domain that resists generalities.

▼▼▼

Why not a popular song extolling New York as the French, with accordions, have so often extolled Paris? Because one can only extol in three-four meter and Americans are too hurried for that. Why *be* in New York? Because it's where you *have* to be: for better or worse it's the center of the universe. Which is why I'll leave soon: I can only feel adjusted off-center.

▼▼▼

If I retire forever to write, does not the very act of writing contradict retirement? How can I wish to chastise Man in words or notes unless *au fond* I want his love? Yet the most agreeable sorrow (the pleasures of pain, the pain of pleasure) is in contemplating the Jersey flats on the train to Philly and wondering where that one reed (that one in billions) will be in a year, in a minute, when the train's gone by.

▼▼▼

Finally heard Liberace. Extraordinary, his fingerwork! He plays all the right notes wrong.

▼▼▼

At loose ends on a Thursday evening, I phone Paul Goodman and invite myself to his group-therapy session. In preparation I wash my hair and don the famous black turtleneck jersey.

Of those eight or ten present, I know only Paul and Sally. . . . Long, very long Quakerlike silence which I finally invade by exclaiming, "Well, since I'm the new one, maybe we could break the ice with someone telling me about the procedure." Silence again, pregnant and sinister. Then Paul speaks. "Ned, the artifice of your social style, your charm, will be your downfall." This drop of blood set the group on me like sharks. At a total loss, I exposed myself to their teeth; mute myself, I was tossed from one stranger's mouth to another; following the leader, they ripped me to ribbons. At which point the session was over. (Charm or not, I *had* been the center of attention!) Then we all had tea and cookies and were filled with fraternal love. No question of a postmortem; only Paul's complaining of always being Father. But he can't have it both ways. As for me, I felt like another Faust: he sells his soul to the devil, then shows his pretty body to Marguerite, who declares, "Oh, I'm sorry, sir, but I prefer older types."

▼▼▼

We can sing it and say so, but how can we be truly glad for what we have or are, since we cannot know until we have not or are not anymore, and then we are no longer glad? Glad for what we've gained? But at this moment we have forgotten yesterday: five minutes after weeping, our tears seem silly. Should a cruel king fall to low place, repent and do good deeds and cry loud and love God, once reascended he will again be cruel. I have never been shown that there is a connection or growth from day to day: it is as easy to forget as remember, as logical to be happy as sad. People say, "I would give my kingdom, my riches, my fame, my soul, for youth and beauty." I have beauty and youth, though how can I know their value? I want a soul, fame, riches, a kingdom.

▼▼▼

A priceless bird hides hardly fluttering in the cage of all our chests, a bird we are not allowed to see until the moment it decides to leave us and fly away forever. How could we have known it was starving inasmuch as we ignored its existence? So as not to become tiresome to others, I oblige them to fall in love with me.

▼▼▼

As I grow I become more and more curious about things, but about people less and less. It's rare that I am not bored by the average person within two minutes and by an intelligent one within two hours (excluding, of course, the physically attractive, who cannot be boring). My only curiosity about fellow humans concerns the waste they make of themselves. Why, I wonder, have even the ugliest been so magnificently constructed: that labyrinth of artery and nerve, more exquisite, fragile, and complex than a beehive's gentle machinery? With what is this mechanism occupied? With sleeping, eating, fornicating, nothing more. Its reason serves solely destruction. Still, it takes nine months of building, more magic and intense than for skyscrapers or ant hills, more patient than for blueprints of pyramids or atom bombs, a muscular waxing, the infinite house of the brain which finally uses about 3 percent of itself. All this emerges, works for years in spite of itself toward a total perfection which will live in the charmed construction incrusting the earth like a transparent jewel. But why, seeing that all this is good for absolutely nothing?

Unimportant that people exhaust their hearts and die at the end of a given time, if only they would ask a question one day in their lives. Yesterday evening I was exposed for hours to the

laughter of five ridiculous girls. Never have I been so bored. One
can say, let them giggle, it's a stage they're going through. But *I*
never went through it; I read and asked questions, not of others
but of myself; the others bored and frightened me. One says too:
they are only girls and require gentlemen, though gentlemen
serve the purpose of their mechanism to even less effect than
animals or vegetation.

▼▼▼

If in half an hour I can make an indelible impression why,
when I go away, must I want to rush back for fear of being
forgotten? Three seconds can inspire a lifetime of loathing.
. . . If a person dies later than he thinks, only a handful more
people will recall him, and already with less mystery. We are
immeasurably more curious about Mozart, Lautréamont,
Maurice Sachs, than about Richard Strauss, Voltaire, Gide.

How, sometimes, could I not compare myself to some god
come down to earth when I look at those about me? Suppose it
were true but that the knowledge for some reason were denied
me: would this keep me from suffering any the less in a contest
for my life? Is the trial of a god like any other when the judges
are blind?

▼▼▼

Donald Gramm and Mattiwilda Dobbs, each in Town Hall
the same week, sang premieres and beautifully for me. Also my
little opera *A Childhood Miracle* received its television debut in
Philadelphia, thanks to Plato Karyanis, Wayne Conner, Dorothy
Krebill, Benita Valenti, and a bunch of instrumentalists from
Curtis conducted by Donald Johanos, all of whom donated their
services. But what else did I get or give in America? Since not a
day passes without history, there are those who say it should be
recorded or lost. But such is a chronicle, not a diary. And history
recorded tonight would not be the same if recorded tomorrow. It
is not what you say but what I say you say.

I drank a lot, was sober a lot, saw a thousand intimate friends, made some new ones, lost old ones, parties, parties, accumulated fans and clarified my situation with the music publishing world, was hated and well-received, grew up and got younger, refound my marvelous mother and father, had a Thanksgiving, a Christmas, and Easter, and no longer believe in my own immortality.

▼▼▼

It is the rainy month of May and next week, after six months, I'm going via London to Marie Laure's in the south of France. I'll be back in the Europe I've missed. If it please God, I'll also be able to miss home.

Is it the memory of New York friends that might make the heart ache? Or will it be rather more difficult to shake the souvenir of sitting in my late-night, early-spring apartment on 23rd, and the window-street sounds of tires on warm-winter New York rain ten stories below?

PART 3

Around the Mediterranean
Summer 1956

*The very act of writing stops thought
by making it dependent on words for its
expression.
We never think that what we think
conceals us from what we are.*

—VALÉRY, *Monsieur Teste*

Hotel Majestic

Beer bullets. I'm in Cannes, again with an awful hangover. Jacques [Février] drove me here yesterday and we dined in Antibes *chez* Marie Blanche de Polignac, after which I got very drunk and was brought back to the hotel at 5 this morning by Tony Pawson's blond friend, who proceeded to beat me up. Now I'm black and blue, alone with a headache, rather gloomy, my hand shakes, throat feels trodden by a Simenon *personnage* wearing spiked shoes on a murderous night *aux* Buttes Chaumont. Am I rewarded by the staggering sumptuousness of these wild scorching September sunsets hurled here by the mistral? It borders on nature's bad taste. A low whistle! I'm in a state of sexual tension which evokes certain memories of the future. It's just seven in the darkening evening and I can't write here any more but must go out into the old quarters and search for odors to excite me. I like to imagine myself admiring the fountain of Toulon's Place Puget and the sudden sweated matty voice of love over a shoulder. But no, I must seek, then avoid it, myself.

A purge. Not the city, it's *myself* I hate in Cannes: sneaking around black corners, shaking and scared (shaking from yesterday's beverage, scared for tomorrow's war), inebriation on the eve of perhaps a new war (I never learn anything either), as if I couldn't remember like yesterday the wars of sixteen and six years ago in the world and in Korea.

Our new religions have an interplanetary inspiration. Mars: the new romance. God of war, this star this month is next door to

Earth. The old say the young have no poetry. Heaven, once a reward, is now a probability. But we are not all so *désabusés* as Françoise Sagan.

▼▼▼

The boredom of completion. When I see the end of a work in progress, when I feel a piano piece under control, I'm no longer interested. This can be dangerous, but I stifle with polishing. My little opera *The Robbers* is two-thirds composed, the remaining third must be the difficult padding of coordination and that is what disturbs my laziness: because it's no longer a question of *souffle,* of inspiration, of pulling the strings all together so that the well-trained marionette can dance his tango without tripping. But when we finally see our destination at the far end of a long bridge, we still have to take the last steps necessary to get there. And these steps are the most fragile: anyone can have ideas, though only *we* can spin them into solid shape.

▼▼▼

Who has a *face* nowadays? My mother, *she* has a face!

▼▼▼

Cannes has always formed the portrait of my dilemma by putting into flesh what I fear. What am I doing in France? Can't I say that for the rest of my life wherever I am?

▼▼▼

Write an opera on Buzatti's *Siete Piani,* or on the suicide pact of *Hôtel du Nord.* Operas should have a nightwatchman (*Meistersinger*) at end and beginning as binding factor. And begin right out (and end) with the *big* aria. Opera for *one* person (on my own imagination).

Write a book (I've begun!). Reverse insanity. For instance, the ending of Paul Gadenne's *Invitation chez les Stirl* might be interpreted by showing that the hero was insane in thinking the others were, and the letter he receives was his own automatic writing composed while asleep. Like *Le voyageur sur la Terre*.

Perhaps I could put this in my book, my opera.

All this, however, is what the French call *bloc notes*, without development. I wish I could keep a more gossipy journal.

▼▼▼

Bad cold, aching back, general fatigue. Wild dream of a razor slicing off the knees of children.

Poulenc's maid speaks of R. the chauffeur: *Vous savez que Monsieur trompe Monsieur*. He's a cross between trumpet and weasel and signs his letters Biquette.

> *Le morse, la fouine et la trompette*
> *Se réunissent en une biquette.*

▼▼▼

> *Pisse-en-lit, pet-de-nonne,*
> *Je suis terriblement putain*
> With a green heart *en etain*
> Which will not know what it has done.

▼▼▼

> What am I choosing!
> On this same road where hand
> in hand I fell in love,
> today I'm cruising.

Because it's Cannes' bullets of gin that riddle me whenever I hit here. Probably I've spent a total of three months in fifteen visits, arriving for a sensual purpose that's usually deflected by my own Venus Fly Trap oozing with booze (what a sentence!), and the trap made of a flesh that I'm told is as far from me as Jekyll from Hyde. And frequently I wonder—on awakening in strange rooms with my mouth like the bottom of a monkey cage—who pulled off those half-remembered crimes last night.

It's 6:30 of a hot Sunday evening. Spent the afternoon at the Plage Sportive with Jean Marais (must he always stay beautiful?), Claude Bénédick, and Philippe Erlanger. Philippe, who neither smokes nor drinks and retires early to work on his Diane de Poitiers, tells me (though I can't remember) that last night I persuaded him to make the rounds by the following logic: *Pourquoi passer la soirée avec une femme morte quand tu peux la passer avec un garçon vivant?*

Now I'm alone writing this on my tan naked lap. Soon I'll go out again. Then tomorrow, passing by Grasse, I'll motor back to the seriousness of Hyères with Marie Laure.

Again it's late afternoon and I'm preparing to leave Cannes where nothing much has happened (except those long pointless misunderstandings with sick Virginia F.) because it's no longer a town of lovers but of whores (mostly Algerians passing themselves off as Spanish), or else I'm just older and beyond the spontaneous honeymoon stage. The sunlight's been massive with spasms of blue. This year the azure coast bores me and I want to work. Excuse me.

▼▼▼

Hyères

For how many years (when practicing the piano) have I thought of myself as subject to this possible torture: obligatory sight-reading when the first false note means death! But who are the judges? Freud was born a hundred years ago today.

▼▼▼

Reading Zweig's weird life of Mary Baker Eddy reminds me of Father's joke of the rabbi explaining about certain of his disciples turned Quaker: "Some of my best Jews are Friends."

Zweig says the man with an *idée fixe* is always the strongest.
Now it seems years since I've been consciously passionate
enough about *one* thing (except myself, in general) to wish to
move worlds through persuasion or acts of conviction. I just
don't care, and am amazed by those who do. This is untrue. But
why did Mark Twain get so excited about Mrs. Eddy making all
that money? Couldn't he foresee Hitler's remarks on the Lie in
Mein Kampf? or the fortune our analysts receive from listening?
(They too wish patients to *earn* the money they pay with.) As
for Zweig, he doesn't once mention Lourdes, or the Congo tribes
who dance impuniously on live coals.

▼▼▼

Suddenly I can stop dead in my tracks alone (so seldom) on a
summer country road at the odor of day's end recognized in a
vanishing flash as the same I knew at sixteen, sixteen years ago,
at Northwestern or with my father in Taxco, where barking and
fountains grew more agitated than bats at sunset. Then I ask
myself why, when I first breathed autumn's new cold or looked
for love in Chicago's parks, couldn't I have savored the firstness
of this love, that cold? It's smells and streets and situations of the
past one misses more than people. Now at thirty-two I know
what I could have done bodily, but I've restrained myself (often
in drink) as an artist more than most, content to know I could
have, or could still. Age is the beginning of the memory of
survived anguish. It is also the awareness of being young.

Responsibility of death. The personal guilt we feel at the
dying of a loved one. Now the boy who knew summer fragrances
was myself, but he's dead (though I didn't kill him). Youth's
departure is a certain dying. We only say "if only" when we
knew the person well. That boy who had all the opportunities he
didn't take: I wonder what I've missed! I can still smell the
clove, carnation, cinnamon, but through a new nose (could it be
then a new smell? after all it's not the same clove, etc.) . . . A

pungent past has nevertheless not kept me from almost finishing the first draft (libretto and music) of my opera *The Robbers*.

▼▼▼

Last night's dream: Oscar Dominguez takes me for a ride in his new flying saucer. We glide low and slowly between tall city buildings whose windows show lamplit scenes of little girls in the white gowns of their first communion. The tail of the vehicle begins to sag and I am frightened. We land on a steep cliff in the forest. Marie Laure is there and takes the hand of Oscar (he's now my father) and they walk off, but I cannot follow because the rocks of the hill give way and I slide back (ugly Oscar was also the violist of the L. Quartet—they once played a work of mine—whose name I've forgotten but whom I thought beautiful in 1947).

▼▼▼

In the water of our morning swim we can already smell the trouble across this small sea, of war in Algeria and Nasser in Egypt.

▼▼▼

When I have written that I've never understood a person's *"caring* enough," I realize now it's because I've never *had* to.

▼▼▼

Miracles happen only in novels. But for long years my life was like a book: I took the fabulous for granted and wishes were realities. Today is today, yet a moment five minutes ago is already memory mingling with fifteen minutes, or weeks, years past, more and more confused. What is present? Or which accomplishment can we enjoy in this second, since it is immediately the past? Death is the straw that broke the camel's back.

▼▼▼

Happiness is a mediocre desire which, if granted, would result in stupor. I don't want happiness, I want the life of curiosity which, mostly, excludes joy.

▼▼▼

The past is more important than the future—I know them both so I can say. It is patience; the future is impulse. The past is also longer—from where we stand today. I live there. Probably I write these words because tomorrow scares me, but anyone can make a future without even waiting, whereas the past (as we see it here) becomes a slow and grand accumulation of uncountable millenniums.

▼▼▼

Am I alive in what I do? Or standing on the outside looking in? (As though what's inside made any difference.) Sleepwalking again. My not caring as to the import of great or small events occurring before or to me (including the happy hypnosis during creative or loving acts) makes me more and more into a sleepwalker. Though I notice that my not caring doesn't prevent me from writing here that I don't care.

I said my life was like miracles in books—taken for granted. Can I have already reached a time when I'm open-mouthed at the memory of afternoons (not so long ago: and past is more than future) when my beauty, conscience and constitution allowed me to drink, in Greenwich Village or St. Germain des Prés, and pick up strangers, so as to have *that* out of the way before evening when I could drink again with real seriousness— and then write symphonies next morning? That's Auric's first recollection of me: in 1949 perched on a midnight stool surrounded by the aged and eager, bright hair askew and wild eyes and beer and cognac flowing fast. And that is how Auric must open his biography of me.

▼▼▼

The bright realization that *must* come just before death will
be worth all the boredom of living.

▼▼▼

Was it Landowska or Genêt who, when someone murmured
"Un ange passe," added: *"Qu'on l'encule!"*? Such libidinousness
I long to retrieve in a few days going back for a little tour of
North Italy, if it still exists. Sadder than *Death in Venice* would
be the death *of* Venice and let's try to visit there at least once
more before we die. Unless we're already the vermin that for
thousands of decades has been clustering with increasing thick-
ness over an expired Earth. If last night I dreamed of being
dead, how can I know that in "reality" the reverse is not true:
that this morning my awakening is a dead man dreaming he is
alive? Have I explained it in music with *Another Sleep?*

▼▼▼

Inconsistency is the diarist's privilege. In three pages I may
contradict what I feel in knowing too well my love affairs and
prefer the harsh suffering of a scene through the keyhole. I keep
making lists of what I must do when I get "there," but once I get
there I forget, the lists being of past desires or acts accomplished.
For instance, I tell myself that when I finally get back to
Chicago (it's been ten years) I'll have to take a look in Tin Pan
Alley on Wabash Avenue, hoping the siege of marihuana and
admiration, benzedrine and beer that carried me through my
seventeenth year will bless me again. Now I'm not even sure
Tin Pan Alley still exists. How well I comprehend sketches of
winged genitals on prison walls! All my daydreams are of former
dissipation.

▼▼▼

Rapallo, August 15 (Assumption of the Virgin)
    We sit at the port cafés and watch faces and faces go by, many
unchanged since Giotto. But this is essentially a vulgar town,

and also noisy (noise of loud Lambrettas, klaxons, strident voices all night): Italy is the noisiest country in the world, and noise for its own sake is my worst torture, probably because I'm a musician and my ears . . . etc . . . Now, Bergamo with its quiet mountain square two days ago (today ago I ache from no sleep) was called by d'Annunzio the city of silence; it's half true: Donizetti died there. I let myself be carried into convulsions by noise. Probably I reason too much to be happy. But physical delights are my shame and ordeal, and even sexuality seems a burden. Maybe these are just Rapallo thoughts because Mary assumes too much today.

Later. We've just been moved to another room on the floor below, having complained about the noise. Darkness into darkness, and I feel quite ill. P.'s at the beach while I lie down in an expensive chamber. We sit on the port watching faces and eat *fragole con panna*. Is it why we're born: to ask no questions? I'm a little disappointed. We're given only so many thrills to a lifetime and (though I try to disguise the fact even to myself) I feel that most of mine are used up. Music interests me less and less (though when I say it I don't wish to be misunderstood; I can still melt, still think that this new room on a quiet court is trembling with Italian guitars) and literature more and more.

My latest affectation is to leave my hair its natural color. It hasn't had a drop of bleach in ten months. Nora Auric (between throws in a game of *pétanque*) says it's the color of better Swiss chocolate with golden highlights. Delights of the pretentious natural: I feel "haloed." I am less sure of myself than most, but I admit what others hide. It is stronger to be loved than to love: it implies *having something*. To love is passive blackmail.

▼▼▼

My first regular drinking was in Duluth, Wis., summer 1939, when Mother and I would have two bottles each of beer at the end of every afternoon. That was sixty-eight seasons ago and the summers float by our stationary bodies (ever more eroded) with

the blandest unconcern. A week ago, I heard Denise Bourdet say
to Jean Godebski (both ending their fifties): *"On dit que la vie
est courte. Ne trouves-tu pas—nous qui avons le même age et
approchons le crépuscule—qu'elle est plutôt longue? Pas trop
longue, mais quand même très longue."* . . . I don't ever want
to say this! In spite of any blasé bitterness I might show today I
want always to think life's great surprise is just around the
corner. After all, I'm a good composer and many know it and this
is a satisfaction which 99 percent of people don't have. I take all
I see and make it my own.

▼▼▼

We went to a revival of *Scarface* and, God, how *démodé* it
was. But Paul Muni is heaven. Look at me in the darling little
sailor hat we stole from Simone Berriau: I'm as cute and *démodé*
as one of those frightful Oranese postcards of lipsticky boys
offering candy roses to insipid damsels. But I liked me that way,
so did Denise (as for hours we went screaming through opera
scores while Simone and sixteen others played poker loudly in
the same room).

This paragraph is a "delight of the pretentious natural." I have
beat André Masson at a game of *boules* (he too knows what
drinking is; his wife is troubled for my future, but he, dear man,
is worried at the small dent he's made. *Ce n'est pas la peine* he
says each day—then paints a picture).

But I'm back in Rapallo (I've never been here before). Now
I'll leave this journal and, during this small vacation away from a
piano, will write some storylets in the beautiful album engraved
with four golden moles (the animal) which Nancy Mitford gave
me.

▼▼▼

Florence
We thought of staying in Viareggio because P. needs seawater
and animation after a year of routine in Dorno, but not only

couldn't we find rooms, the town turned out to be a vulgar
steaming wound like a Texas outpost overrun with tourists. So
we continued on to Florence last night and here we are in the
Pensione Aprile. Far from the sea, even this paradise swarms like
the tower of Babel and we've just bumped into Alvin Ross, who's
coming here to dine with us. He tells sadly of the death last
month of Alan Ross MacDougall; the swirl of those Drossie
Restaurant days revives to overflowing here in the Piazza della
Signoria as Harold Norse and others from then come by, all
older, to interrupt the meditations in our peach ice cream. And
floods of August visitors who cannot look at a great work except
years later in their own snapshots (when a masterpiece rises up
their eyes go down on the camera). Dougy is dead and nothing's
static. When people ask me if my year of psychoanalysis did me
"any good," I say: "How can I know really? Since I was a year
older at the end." Was it analysis or the passing weeks that
changed me (if I changed)? I'm a new person with different
problems every day; analysis tries to remold the same old lump of
clay as though time were static. Of course maybe it *is* (depend-
ing from where you look) but not on a level which concerns
these doctors.

▼▼▼

Any cloister anywhere with weeds, abandoned, makes a vision
of peace. . . . My health feels *scabreuse* again. The usual
hemorrhoid condition. I am never comfortable. . . . Deceits of
meaning, tricks on the ear: as a kid in French class I used to hear
in "Frère Jacques," the line *sonnez les matines* as: Sonny laid
Matina! . . . Does *dégoût* = *d'égout?* . . . This afternoon
we're going for tea at Harold Acton's La Pietra.

▼▼▼

Tea turned out to be cocktails (I had lemonade), H. Acton's
Jamesian mother, and the most beautiful gardens in the world
(with a gardener still more beautiful than his roses). The roses

were haunted. The old mother said: "All *my* friends are dead!";
and Acton looks like Henry Cowell. When I asked him (just to
be pleasant) if he knew my friend Douglas C., he answered: "In
my house don't mention the name of that loathsome hypocritical
snake" etc. . . . The same thing happened a few hours later as
we were dining (in Harry's Bar) with John Pope Hennessey, of
whom I asked Violet T.'s phone number: "Why do you want to
call *that* stupid pretentious lady?!" Really, rich English art
historians put one in a *situation fausse*. It's so hot you can't
breathe. This afternoon we leave for Venice.

▼▼▼

Venice—Pensione Paganelli

Why does Venice seem always to mean the death of someone?
Why don't maniacs more frequently put rocks on tracks to cause
train disasters (it's so easy) like the Hungarian lunatic who used
to stand off in the woods to applaud the mass of twisted steel and
broken bodies he'd just caused? The endless tunnels Italian
railroads go through, as aggravating as a woman's purse! So I
bought *Time* and read it from cover to cover as is my habit once
a year (never oftener) and was struck in the eyes by the "Mile-
stone" column announcing the end of John Latouche at thirty-
eight. As one does in such cases, I let the train clatter on and
closed my eyes to review a relation with Touche from the time
we first met one dawn of 1944 at Valeska Gert's on Bleecker
Street, till our last meeting two or three months ago when he
talked (in the French style) to me and Larry Josephs late into
the night. During these twelve years he was the symbol of
immoderate freshness in a country where assembly-line resem-
blance seems the rule. The attack on his heart was only appro-
priate (I hate moderation in any form), but the attack on our
own provides a sad and damaging shock. *Où sont les nègres
downtown?* . . . Poetically speaking, growing up is mediocrity.
And this week more artist friends have died never having had

time to realize they'd grown up: Professor Kinsey, Brecht, Jackson Pollack, Papini. Now Oscar tells us that Dominguin has returned to the bullring. How admirable. Becoming adult is acceptance of going no farther. Where is the use of saying I have all, money, love, fame, etc.? Rip it down and start over like a spider aiming higher.

▼▼▼

Rushing with Jean Stein from the Piazza toward the Accademia bridge, we came to Mary McCarthy, whom I do not know. The thrill at witnessing the famous hairdo is that she's good and I'd dream of librettos from her if I weren't now making my own.

A month ago I'd written in the new notebook:

"The Fall days known as 'glorious' were over." McCarthy's chapter-start could only be by a woman (such an attitude from, say, Thoreau, is unimaginable; even James would not have conceived it just this way), but a very special woman, for Millay might have banally declared: "The glorious Fall days were over." It's the word *known* that indicates the cold avoidance of romanticism, i.e. the Fall days are glorious to others but the reaction's only known (not felt) by us intellectuals who find beauty in rarer style rather than in Nature's dubious daily taste. No male writer, however effeminate, need prove his maleness, so may be as perfumed as you please. But women just can't win: their style's either so feminine only they could have made it, or so masculine only they could have made it. ("No one's going to call *me* a 'woman author'!") Does McCarthy realize that her sentence, nevertheless, could be the opening of a sonnet?

▼▼▼

Dream. We were a slippery gang of boys, eleven, seven, naked as a sky slashing in a country lake. Our voices not yet changed squealed like girls' speeding down the slick tin toboggan flashing

into water—the echo of our child-voice lashed the lake with a
shudder of pleasure: we were clean American Protestant Youth.
Now lying weary on the still naked bank we (being clean)
began mutually to clean our ears. Those of us who didn't bite
our nails could dig out with a little fingertip nice globes of
reddish wax; the others managed with toothpick and cotton.
Picnic of hairless bodies glowing sleeker than pears on a hill. In
cleaning one's own ear it is easy to gauge the recesses, the un-
beat drum, the necessary depths. Somebody else's cave though
makes as slippery a danger as our lake. Suddenly among us stood
a sailor. No one had seen him appear, he was just there, a little
sad and virile, soiled and unsmiling. How were we meant to act
before the adult whose muscular neck burst tired from a cloth? It
was known in a look that I must clean his ears and, standing on a
stool beside him, I began. Here I am faint at the fragrance of a
grown-up man whose caramel biceps rich and thick could smash
my veins. Odor of muscle. Sniffing the oil I can't comprehend I
shove the cotton toothpick into a wax like cheese. I do not know
how far to go, no one says Stop or even seems to see. With a
thrust the drum is split and the sailor in slow motion falls like a
jelly. The children all have disappeared, and across the cadaver I
perceive a dark tall woman who evidently is not disapproving
though she doesn't smile.

  I see myself as others see me, for I can quit my stationary body
and walk around myself examining at ease this immobile boy
sitting in the country church, and sitting on as others file out
forever into sun. But is it seeing myself: one part observing
another? Anyway there's a child in black short pants there
gritting his teeth or running his tongue about his lips craving,
craving with twitched mouth but riveted to his seat. Three: like
a double exposure I can see the same child rising from himself
(leaving me the sitter nevertheless) and straining toward the
open door through which he even cannot pass. Here it's white
and clean; out on the church lawn is laughter. The boy sitting
sees all, would like and would be welcome to participate in the

happy flashing through the door—a tongue sweating. Still, he remains.

▼▼▼

Why does mediocrity have that nervous laugh? Those overheard beach conversations when someone says, "It's a hot day"—and then snickers. Or something equally banal which just isn't funny. Does this dumb unfelt giggle impose assurance onto insufficiency? Or is it a groping toward poetry (if you'll pardon both terms)? There should be a prison for the mediocre, for those who laugh too much, who overreact. But then of course there'd be so few people left.

▼▼▼

A man who had tired of this same view of the rainbow longed for visions at a new angle. But when he gave his soul to the devil and stood looking from where we cannot see, he knew that on the rainbow's other side there was just more of the same color as though his mirrored self were observing a live body in reverse.

▼▼▼

Kenneth Pitchford writes from Seattle that the *Black Mountain Review* considers me the worst American composer. Not just second-rate or bad, but the *worst!* Is being thus singled out as unique true glory?

▼▼▼

An intelligent fool, I am also *une allumeuse* setting traps which catch only myself while other hunters vanish and leave me agape. "For once I'm telling the truth," he lied.

▼▼▼

Hyères, September
And drums and beasts and fancy gowns. A week ago I got back from North Italy in a plane so small it was like riding a

kettledrum into France. Returned to Hyères just as Denise and Jacques returned from Bayreuth full of *The Master Singers*. Jacques breaks the piano daily practicing Ravel's Concerto—the one for two hands I played at Northwestern in 1940.

Autumn seems now to have come with dark winds and cold incessant rain keeping us indoors in bare feet after a troubled summer of restraint. But maybe it is just this restraint I half-involuntarily self-impose which brings out the best in whatever work I may accomplish. This of course is balanced by the artifice of my famous binges; I so seldom abandon myself to joy and fun (relaxed and natural) that I'm capable of realizing I've *forgotten* to get drunk, *forgotten* to make love with myself or go to the bathroom, as though it were forgetting to buy a loaf of raisin bread. But I prefer my intimacies by correspondence, am embarrassed (no: annoyed) by time-consuming actuality. One can be tongue-tied with exasperation at a thumb sliced by a rim of paper.

▼▼▼

I am reading a history of Quakerism (Howard Brinton), though concentration is dubious when each morning the news of Nasser's Egypt appears even heavier. Actions seem arbitrary, pointless, and a coming war feels almost aimed against me personally. When I was a child I thought "growing up" would supply rational answers to the dangerous games of war which I could not yet understand. Now I am adult and the accepted contradictions of propaganda are just as baffling: overnight the Japanese (whom we were required to hate by caricature in the early '40s) became our brothers, the German changed from ghoul to angel, North Koreans were bad and South Koreans good (simple as the nursery rhyme), and Russians are dumb when they show themselves intelligent. I didn't, and do not, comprehend. "Thou shalt not kill," we were taught, so how, how do we reconcile that command with compulsory military training?

All this was complicated a few days ago by the sun producing an explosion stronger than a trillion atomic bombardments, giving that star this morning a silver instead of gold look. But of what consequence are children's questions?

▼▼▼

Where today is that slip of paper mislaid for twenty years on which Jean Harlow wrote her autograph? Burned? Then are the ashes fertilizing graveyards? Jean's long dead and her celluloid's yellowing. My loves for music and movies were (still are) joined and confused as Siamese twins. Soon I wrote fan letters to John Alden Carpenter whose replies I treasured. Then suddenly (was it only yesterday?) Ravel died. Twelve years old! Twelve years are a great many when they're all you have. When I was twelve in 1936 that distance from my birthday seemed as far as it does from today because I had fewer comparisons. What the French called *le recul du temps* is only relative, because the stretch from my birth to my third birthday was so vast I couldn't even remember it. And night before last seems ages ago when you're only one day old. (Or one day dead.)

At fourteen I knew by heart the poems of Cummings. Could I arise today in Quaker meeting and discuss the pacifist use of his personal pronoun "i"? Or at least if we must capitalize it, let's do the same with You.

▼▼▼

Tuesday I take the Mistral for Paris and a brand-new summer is gone gone gone. I've read fifty books, slightly traveled in strange towns, written stories and an opera (though not orchestrated), gleaned and forgot, feared a war, praised *Le Balcon,* learned Catalan and Provençal, and visited the ruins of Edith Wharton's nearby mansion barefoot with Nancy Mitford who doesn't like Americans. I awaken daily filled with morning sickness like a pregnant woman: it must be a holdover from Cannes, or the shock of Henri *le maître d'hôtel's* statement on

Charles de Noailles, or my heart touched by Dior's praises of
Chicago, or embarrassment at the proud gardener's very crippled
son who writes awful music and wants to join the Société des
Auteurs. Now Yves Nat too has died. Maggy has finally renounced me and married Richard Fisher after sixteen years of
whirlwind courtship. And Xenia (Shirley Gabis Rhoads) has a
baby boy. But I go on forever. My Second Symphony, written
last winter in New York, just had its premiere with sweet
reviews in La Jolla. And the First Symphony (1949) will have
its eighth performance this month in Oslo.

▼▼▼

3:30 A.M. (*aux cabinets*). Went to bed sick and now am
sicker with surprise. Sleep is a noisy ocean which I hope to cross
from night to morning and arrive cured.

Next day: I must stay in bed, an olfactory kingdom. Lily and
Marie Laure stuff me with laxatives, prunes, blue suppositories.
Outside it's hot and bright. I'm feverish and forceless.

▼▼▼

A journal gives a false perspective, for sometimes the entries
grow congested as accordion pleats, while other times the spacing
is wide enough for storms to enter and evaporate. For instance,
the sixty or so pages of the present book cover more than a year
while my first volumes were stuffed with weeks. But in flipping
through the leaves we often disregard a date so that living seems
a matter of daily crises.

Put down the book now, look up, imagine that what you've
been reading has become real: that a burglar will crawl through
the window, or that you will truly have to face a world battle
unless you curl up into a shell of insanity which in any case
means change.

PART 4

Paris and New York
Autumn 1956

God knows it's little use;

God knows I have spent ages
peering like a stuffed owl
at these same blank pages
and, though I strained to listen,
the world lay wrapped with wool
far as the ends of distance.

And what do I hear today?
Little that sounds mine—
                    —W. D. SNODGRASS

Returned to Paris night before last and immediately had my first *cuite* (with Elliott and Kenneth Anger, who met me at the train) getting *that* out of the way! Yesterday, the long sordid promenade of recuperation, and a movie (Renoir's *Eléna et les Hommes*—boring fun), great fatigue. Today routine begins. I'm writing naked in a sunny window. Now on the telephone I make a hundred dates (both G. B. Shaw and Freud are a hundred), particularly with Tom Keogh, whom Marie Laure's commissioning to do the sets and costumes for *The Robbers*, but also my dear Jean Leuvrais (he's in Julien Green's *l'Ombre* which I'll see Sunday), Gary Graffman, and Ninette of the Parc Montsouris.

▼▼▼

A visit to Victor Hugo's house, now a museum in the Place des Vosges, where in the folly of his dotage he carved furniture —*with his teeth!*

Cocteau once said that Hugo was a madman who thought he was Hugo. Do I think I'm Ned Rorem? No longer.

▼▼▼

Certain former winds passing with a cool touch of the almost old-fashioned can nevertheless intone in a manner unbearably sensual. For instance, Debussy's *Jeux*, or *Ces Plaisirs* of Colette, which I've just been reading. No word is out of place nor superfluous and the images spill overlapping and silver with her polished unrestraint.

She never drank, having that writers' curiosity for observation which only sobriety can provide. My drinking is an order perhaps, and part of a larger self-organized control; however, boredom (which only "intellectuals" can feel) and big cities and nervousness before others lead me daily, at cocktail hour from 6 to 8, through an anguished struggle to which I fall victim at least one time in seven (too often!) and awaken with the *bonne mine de la fièvre* that vanishes the second day and leaves me a ghost. That is when I walk the streets, too tired to consider anything but my body.

And that is when I learn the language of the spider nests (known also as confessionals and centipedes), so-called by myself because of the female thinker in the middle, legs apart, awaiting the gobble on which the whole organism is focused: *Occupe-toi de mon maximum,* or perhaps: *j'enfile mon fils,* followed by (in a different script): *tu n'en es pas le seul!* Let's place a silent camera well-aimed in these domains and leave it twenty-four hours; then (with adroit cutting, *bien sûr*—not just *anyone* appeals to us) show the results some Sunday at the Cineclub accompanied by Debussy's *Reflets dans l'Eau.* And why, after all (with *Feuille de Rose*), doesn't Dior use "blow" as a cologne title? *On ne rentre pas avec qui l'on sort* is a slogan of the upper classes who attend the theater with a white-minked lady and are sometimes written about in readable novels; but, to my conscious knowledge, it never happens to *me,* and this, *enfin,* is what my journal concerns.

▼▼▼

Bright blue smoky clean brisk autumn temperature which every year has that fragrance of troubled delight, and means "going back to school" in a bonfire, while I see that little boy, as through the wrong end of a telescope, growing smaller and smaller in whirling leaves—but for once it's rather pleasant. In less than two weeks I'll be thirty-three—and next February 23, 1957, I'll be a third of a century old!

The remorse I still (it's physical rather than moral, I suppose) feel from my *cuite* of Thursday shows always that *au fond* I am really a middle-class American. The morose and agreeable vegetation from a hangover in the wombish bed a bit humid with the comforting smell of my own fingernails, perspiration and yesterday's breath—a false hunger from which I get up and go to the baths Rue Cambronne where I soothe a smashed knee. Only ivy-league babies make rubbing love.

▼▼▼

Ernie is of a rare yet solid breed: the annoyingly delightful not-too-young expatriate sensitive lush living off an untalented intellect and a small but regular allowance from somewhere in Vermont. He is ubiquitous: you leave him dead drunk at the Flore, take a plane to Venice, rush to Harry's Bar, and somehow he's already there, dead drunk—and has seen all the movies. So you ask him how they are—there being a local rush on old Dietrich–Garbo–Davis films. "Why, they're having a George *Brent* festival!" . . . I mention all this as introduction to his disappearance. Because his passive ingratiating presence hasn't been about lately, and when you're not trying to work his bitchery is always welcome.

Well, this afternoon at the Montana, wretchedly hungover, I was sitting alone having a pick-me-up, dizzily dried-out and susceptible: even the ashtray looked menacing. In walks Heddy De Ré, plump in her jeans and still fresh after last night. (How does she *do* it! By putting Privine in her eyes.) "Have you heard about Ernie?" she asks eagerly. "You know where he's been these last months? Killed!" And she has the nerve to tell me, in my condition, of his murder in San Francisco: two drunk sailors tied him face down on the bed, thrust his curling iron into the rectum, attached the electricity, and vanished into the night singing sea chanties. Next day he was found in black powder.

▼▼▼

Women as fish on fire. Sapphire sharks. Flaming water. Ocean of glaciers, a shifting of blood on the globe, black bleeding glaciers, so nothing stays static.

▼▼▼

For *The Robbers* I want an opening curtain (as beautiful as Picasso's for *Parade*), a scrim through which, after the shriek, the three men will be perceived half-holding-up the corpse which they let fall gradually as this inner curtain is slowly raised and the light grows for the first words. And at the end I thought that after the leader says "help!" and during the final bars, the door might open slowly, but the curtain drops before we can see who is about to enter.

▼▼▼

The delicious simple one speaks: "I don't believe you really had that dream. You must have made it up." What is the difference?

▼▼▼

Midnight, in bed with a cold. I'm daily more and more obsessed with sex. My fancies fly to any doorknob, drop of water, loaf of bread. Yet public baths and casual contacts (so very casual!) leave me toughened and unsatisfied, wanting the personal smash of lips and arms. But found, why do I let them go? Why do I stand them up? There in a line, swarthy, loving me, they were everything I pretended to desire. Why then did I ever let them all get away?

I have a conscious dread of my own intoxicated spells whose approach I feel as a kind of awful duty required, like epilepsy, by my demon half.

I wish my work weren't more important than my play.

These three paragraphs seem like uncontrolled conflicts. But if I'm as advanced as the baby who throws his all-day sucker out

of his crib and then cries for it back, is it balanced by the restraint in my drinking knowledge? And I *do* wish I knew how to
play really well, and not just how to work *fairly* well. These
tedious eternal Journal Queries.

▼▼▼

Last week at Jean-Pierre Marty's: birthday gift in the form of
a thunderbolt. I am in love again for the first time! Exuberant
need to giggle and screech. The bloated earth already seems too
small for the sky which stabs drab Avenue Marceau with yellow
rubies although for weeks the fall sun's been typically tight over
Paris. Yet my childish heart claps as though spring had come
bringing the urge to utter those same old corny lines—but to
new ears. *Oh Claude, Claude, Claude, Claude, Claude, je t'aime
encore plus que tu ne m'aimes!*

▼▼▼

—*N'ébourriffez pas mes cheveux.*
—*Pourquoi pas? Tu as toute la vie pour te les repeigner.*

▼▼▼

Time Out for the Dying, Pleasures for the Dying. Because for
a person in any way condemned, living takes sharper meanings.
His letter might read: "I cannot say I take 'time out' to write
you; the very writing is a pleasure in this time-limit of which
each second I protract into an immediate memory. For the
remainder of my stay is so short that I allow no waste and am
aware, joyously, of every hour. No sound or color, nothing of
taste or touch goes by unnoticed. What a luxury!"

▼▼▼

Claude woke me up to say Hungary's been invaded by Russia,
they're massacring people right and left, all Europe's threatened.

▼▼▼

This afternoon Maurice Gendron, just returned from Vienna, tells of that city filled with bulldozers arriving from Budapest covered with blood. I don't understand.

▼▼▼

Halloween

Winter's awfully here with another war seeming well on its way like a searchlight wail of mammoths straining the sky. All around in Africa and Hungary is such positive and bleeding unrest. I'm scared. Is it any wonder I always say: sleep is no waste? More than ever in this week that I've been thirty-three I need nine dream hours from which to wake and learn again secrets from a spidery world (language of the spider nests). Everyone's glued to his radio, newspapers, words heard on a bus through chilling fog that now covers Paris.

▼▼▼

Gieseking has died. The last issue of *Folder* printed three songs: one by John Latouche, one by Ben Weber, one of mine. Now Touche is dead. Which one will be next? Who will come third? and how? When I was your age I understood everything, got the point, had all the answers; today at my age I understand nothing, don't get the point, have no answers.

Lightning changes, politics switch overnight, revolutions all about, and discontent, tension, fright, depression, sorrow, nerves, war scare. Yet out of my window the streets look just the same: leaves fall, the sun sets, children laugh as though nothing were up. Last night, dining uncomfortably, Rue Mazarine, with Elliott Stein, Henri, and Kenneth Anger, the strain of conversation terminated thus:

Henri: *Enfin, on verra bien.*
Me: *On verra mal.*
Elliott: *On verra pas!*

Nobody talks but of the stupid crumble, and my only hope, notes, this little book, so perishable. Of all nervous diseases, hysteria (as in Ionesco's theater) bores me the most.

▼▼▼

Another afternoon with Alice Toklas. This woman still in the company of *that* woman whose power was such she even influenced her predecessors (as I'm influenced by the future). So many of us, and even dogs, have survived the rise and fall of Hitler. She loves politics but I hate them. Again the near-dying. Her explanation (not mine) of the American male's eternal youth is that, wanting to be like his neighbor, he's unable to change (whereas the Frenchman, for conversational exercise, on purpose takes a contrary viewpoint). As for American women she says merely: "Yes, *aren't* they though!" And also, "Quaker? it's the only thing to be!" How much farther does she have to go, and will we meet again? Correspondence is a pleasure of the deaf. Is it why, as a musician, I write so many letters?

▼▼▼

Played my opera for Poulenc today and he says to call it *The Novice*. I will. Sauguet, *lui*, tells me my ideal opera subject now should be an American comedy based on the Marx Brothers' *A Night at the Opera*.

▼▼▼

André Fraigneau and Sherban Sidéry, bored by my singing of *The Robbers*, swoon at Mattiwilda Dobbs' record of *Pippa's Song*. But the opera, I tell them, has just as gorgeous a vocal line. God, but I'm credulous, and never cease to be astonished at how everyone's out for himself: Marie Powers, Françoise Sagan, Ella Fitzgerald, these ladies (and each, except Marie, with a special poignant surprise of her own) have no time for the works of others. The tedium of arrival. I lose ambition. I drink as a robot wound up whose springs go wild from tension. It's regular. I'm *pince-sans-rire* (they tell me), passing spare moments these perilous days in making narcissistic collages which I mail unsolicited to certain friends and friends of friends.

▼▼▼

In a week Claude and I go to the Netherlands. I've never been there for tulip time, but in November it's ideal honeymooning because of an unchallenging blandness, a sort of Germany *manqué*. The men all look like theological students and the women like gym teachers. Six years ago with Julius Katchen I remember those vast long surrealist snowy beaches covered not with winter swimmers but with ladies in muffs drinking foamy chocolate, and Russian wolfhounds in sleighs.

▼▼▼

Amsterdam, Hotel Victoria
Hardly the moment to write in diaries: time's suspended. But last night in The Hague we went to hear Monteux conduct Irma Kolassi's *Schéhérazade*. Claude was moody throughout: time's too precious for us to spend concertizing. Afterward I went alone backstage, telling Claude to wait at the bridge. I returned to find him vomiting copiously into the canal. Why, why? Because in the morning, after a big Dutch cheesy breakfast, as he sat on the great Dutch toilet thumbing through this diary, he came across the cruel couplet of a few weeks ago (—*N'ébourriffez-pas mes cheveux* . . .) and felt it applied to him. Tomorrow France and reality again.

▼▼▼

Who walks into the Montana last night but Ernie! I'm stupefied, and somehow embarrassed. "I thought you were—" He comes to my aid: "Dead? Yes, gossip *is* unclear at times, isn't it?"

▼▼▼

Since birth I don't recall a month the world could enjoy the ease of peace. It's a generation enveloped by dangerous dispute. But with what necessary quickness we grow used to calamity! For instance, now we take in our toughened stride Hungarian news, and African, the worst is at our door, *tant pis,* when only twenty days ago we shook. But I work, go on. If I don't live on today's earth, when, on which one, *will* I?

It is snow time without snow: a rather blurred desire for flakes through which gray sun rays come lying onto this page. It is also Monday. We were in Holland, Claude and I, a week ago four nights and days. Must happiness be paid for? The radio is spouting horrors about new concentration camps in Egypt, the kidnapping of Nagy, the shock of hate all over, the exodus into Austria, and crimes, while I dream on of the movies in Amsterdam and scarves and pastries, of the *zeebad* honeymoon in the Kurhaus Hotel at Scheveningen near The Hague, a wintry actionless dream of Dutch beaches, that country scraped clean of character offering the ideal anonymous décor for new lovers passing tens of hours in bed. Nail me to this wave. Must this fragile book too vanish? Can the dead fall in love with the yet-unborn? Let us be thankful we're of the same generation. Or look at poor old Joan Crawford in *Autumn Leaves,* the poor young murderess of *The Bad Seed:* these American age phenomena are passing simultaneously now on Champs-Élysées screens. Cinema in general pleases me so much more than theater. Like panic, it is the art of my time.

▼▼▼

Last week when Dora Maar finished her final and best in a series of charcoal drawings for which I was the model, I gave the beautiful result to Claude to have photographed and framed. He forgot it in a taxicab! No frantic searching of the Bureau des Objets Trouvés has availed and I'm as sick from this loss as Gide from his burnt letters. Yet I'd rather have Claude than Dora's picture, and wonder how in five days I can leave a *garçon* who strongly looks after my weary gums in his midnight dental office *à la* Villette. But I will leave, and his drawer stuffed with my daily *pneumatiques* speaking of a good love time. Nothing is harder with these sentiments than to write convincingly what one does not feel: the disorder and lonely panic of a shopgirl's love letter is more moving than the greatest sonnet using the same words in different order. In speech anyone can lie well with a manner of eyes or tears. Writing has no sound (we only imagine it has the sound we imagine it has). My letters have no lies; it can be seen; he will know it. Nevertheless I will leave.

Speaking of eyes, a ragged lady accordionist yesterday in the Place de la République had a pair of false ones in dolly-staring glass all immobile in a scorched face. Why? Because this shock inspires no pity, and the blind have other means.

▼▼▼

December 9, on board the Queen Mary

A week on water is about as far as you can go in boredom. Great creative plans projected for just these days of irresponsible bliss all fall to monotonous pieces which regroup themselves into a portrait of waiting, waiting for the meal gong or the next movie. At least this time I have a cabin alone and not with my usual four octogenarians who fart and snore and leave the light on all night and crowd ill-tempered around the morning mirror in their dirty socks. So my cabin has grown into a world apart where I keep myself from the sunny Atlantic and write to Claude for hours on end, playing "the mysterious passenger" who talks to no one and refuses the intrigue of the evening Bingo game.

Always more, how I shun the ordinary. I want to be the luxury of lives, and have a lover be my long dessert. Is it why I've so often been divorced? I won't now believe that Claude's familiarity too will tarnish.

If you take the No. 75 bus to the end of the line you will go up a street in the 10th Arrondissement called *La rue de la grange aux Belles*. Here is where I choose to live with all it implies of love and slaughter. Oh, I am devoured by the greediest masochism and want it, want it four hours *à bouche pleine* before you pin to his dying the glad shaky moth. *N'est pas aimé qui veut.* Is a man who "possesses" another, twice a man? Or the contrary? It depends from where you look. If you're on the bottom, crushed, back toward the bed, don't forget your gaze is skyward, that the bottom is the bass, the very foundation on which a male's melody role is constructed.

▼▼▼

From 1925 to 1950 American women have been Mae West and Martha Graham, Billie Holiday and Marilyn Monroe, Djuna Barnes and Maria Callas (who just makes the time limit). The first two are conquerors, the next are victims, the last seem troubadours for the others, and all grow immediately legendary.

▼▼▼

Since tomorrow, Friday, at dawn, we are—twenty-four hours late—to arrive in New York (where Jean Stein has found me an apartment in the East 60's, of all places), I may as well put a few words here this evening since I probably won't be writing again for months.

The whole trip's been a bore: a sort of *huis clos* on the waves transporting; but a calm preparation to the ambitious frenzy waiting.

All the time's passed in moping for C. When in love I oblige everyone else to love my lover too, and hate them for it. People don't turn to look at me as much as they used to. Nothing is aliver than falling in love, but, when over, limper than a dead fish. The contrast is more than black to white. Is sleep a waste? Never.

Who has the right to camp? It's a matter of *seeing* yourself

doing what you *know* you're doing—like having the right to say
"Moonlight Sonata" . . . (The third convolution, etc.) Also
Rae Robertson just died. I got in at the end. Because, with his
wife Ethel Bartlett, he recorded my old Siennese *Sicilienne*
about seven months ago.

Adieu little friends: Vera Korène, with your husky sapphic
contralto and your guitar on a couch; good Heddy *de mon
époque Heddy* never to be refound; Harold Acton, Roger
Peyrefitte. Hello again: Greta Keller and Carlo Van Vechten.
Some, but not all, of you are part of me. John Lehmann sent my
stories back saying "they just aren't very good." I want newer
smells and wider flowers, a life in the country with fresh eggs
and work near to Claude, for whom I compose letters I'd hesitate
to reproduce in a diary because they are too right and true and
dirty and loving and unstyled and selfless and mean. I am a
musician after all.

▼▼▼

New York City, January, 1957
Why? I have everything, I have you. Why then? Yet hardly a
day goes by when at bedtime—for reasons unknown to myself—
I don't contemplate suicide. It's the kind of extravagant romanticism I should have shed ten years ago before my excess forces
could tire of unnecessary thoughts. Now today is again in a
worldly state of useless chaos surrounded by expensive mistakes,
and tomorrow so quickly grows into yesterday that I feel a
prisoner between two seasons: no place.

I've been back in New York a month and there's bright
electric snow with a thousand friends. Where could I rather be
without love? Americans penetrate the heavens but not the
earth; they don't know how to copulate, but build skyscrapers.
The rich here, as everywhere, seem to have that "misery prior-
ity" which makes them ignore a poet as though everyone didn't
really love everybody for at least one ulterior motive. I am
mondain but not very sociable (there *is* a difference).

Having crossed an ocean again, now, at thirty-three, I begin to situate myself. At that age, by standards here, one ought to have "arrived," and of course I have come where I've come, not yearning for the old times of discovery (Carl Ruggles' *Sun Treader*), but still not caring much. The concrete 12-toners think they are recovering primary sound, but they are only uncovering surface noise. Ansermet said the other day that music isn't concerned with *sound,* but with *notes.* Etcetera. Still I'm not interested. Oh, I phone and orchestrate, write letters and go out scrounging, don't drink much and lament over money, don't feel like composing but don't talk about it. Actually the miracle moment I'm waiting for (thank God we must always have this) is Claude's arrival in seventeen days. And now I already feel better.

▼▼▼

When I am in love I must gobble and rip, demoralize and entangle, ensnare and devour, desecrate and be enveloped, snip and run off, suck and weave webs, be stroked and be penetrated, become idiotic, shrieking, followed, coy and mean, scared but destructive and ferociously passive. These are needs, with traps that help work. The moment has almost come. Let us orchestrate.

Taking it out of your *braquette,* and feeling as the crazed lioness in the arena who, with a brief flashing claw, rips open a martyr's chest and sweeps forth a bleeding lung, a heart, steaming guts, and devours them. You've spoken of the ecstasy of torture which I fear so. Being in love and mutually, I place it above all art and reason, blush that you understand and condone my needs, and even offer to aid, excited. Adults keep children's sillinesses but not their wisdom. I'll make your triangle tingle, or see that noisy sleep which sings into the kingdom of a bed.

▼▼▼

Could Rebecca West's *The Return of the Soldier* make an opera? Is there a letter scene? or colored streamers? or people in disguise?

Mexico's poverty is Catholic dirt, and that is why it depresses us more than Morocco. There's nothing in the Bible when you really need it. Elliott Stein to the Mona Lisa: "Wipe that smile off your face."

▼▼▼

American Negroes since the Puerto Rican emigrations have lifted themselves up a rung. A taxi driver, black as coal, will now say: "You can't move a foot without bumping into some Spic!"

▼▼▼

Tomorrow Claude comes. Anemones fill the room.

The French preoccupation with God and the devil now seems both farcical and humorless. If the devil exists, if he's as powerfully sly as Catholics believe, isn't it possible that their image of God is Satan in disguise? After all, the Church's history was more diabolically bloody than any other.

Situation: the Protestant in a confessional.

▼▼▼

Weak men are so often portrayed by strong women: Sebastian, Octavian, l'Aiglon. Why not Joan of Arc played by a man? And I like Félix Labisse's notion of Hamlet acted by the dwarf Piéral. Who decides? Couldn't Cleopatra be done convincingly by Tony Perkins, Blanche du Bois by Edwige Feuillère, or Macbeth by Marilyn?

▼▼▼

Just as the emphases of musical generations alternate forever between contrapuntal and harmonic (meaning sacred and profane, and these in turn alternate between church and street, and sometimes it's street songs which are canonic while the mass grows lumpy), so society's sexuality is covert or overt, Victorian or Bacchanalian. Today music is contradictorily contrapuntal (holy) in contradistinction to our uninhibited sex. Though really there's no difference, really both are eternally equally present.

▼▼▼

He came and stayed three weeks and left. *Quel gâchis!* The bottom has fallen out of my life.

PART 5

Letter to Claude: New York and Paris

March–May 1957

Ce n'est pas dans Montaigne, mais dans moi, que je trouve tout ce que j'y vois.

—PASCAL

Cher Claude,

You've come and gone.

I write to you now in my journal because I no longer dare speak. You've imposed a straitjacket, though if I could get out I'd be more useless than before: suffering only seems unreasonable to those who cause it. Yet haven't I in these very pages exclaimed that hysteria (as in Ionesco's theater) is the nervous disease that most galls me?

And I'm writing in French, because when I think of you it's in that language, and I think of you always. To hear it now hurts the heart. I've tried to rid my room of your traces, but go into the city only to find you there again in fifty souvenirs. I can't stop shaking. Every morning at the mailbox, knowing there'll be no letter, fearing what you might or might not write. All composers, like dentists, become, through the years and unbeknownst to themselves, sadistic, by dint of doing a job that obliges people to shy away. I reread new meanings into everything, from your first impotence of last October to your indifference of last month. Was it that in having, you no longer wanted? You said you'd loved me in secret four years before we met, for *my* indifference, but wasn't the result more conquest than affection? It's harder to investigate the shadows of one's own soul than of someone else's, but we've got to try, or we'll never know each other (though must people know each other?). You criticized me too much for me not to suspect a lack also *chez toi.* How many times a day you'd ask: "What are you thinking about?" You must contribute

65

too a bit toward something you've half-invented. A touch of tenderness doesn't necessarily imply *ménage*. This apparent lack in you is what gives rise to a hazy suspicion about your very nature.

Once you wrote that I belonged to you. That meant ownership, not affection. To be jilted unexpectedly is rough. It's crazy what two people will do bad to each other, as though the world weren't going to anyway. Flay each other without anesthetic. I've never been left before. Yes, my vanity's touched: why not? Happiness is made mostly of pride. But I'm sad by what will have been errors in judgment, in having selected someone unable to get over the shock of clay feet, the vague conception of what virility is supposed to be in anyone. Thank God I'll have learned it soon enough to be able to find a taste for life again—though not soon enough to have had heart bruised or ideas altered about what used to be called human relations. Now you lower your eyes before the deluge you've provoked.

I tell you all that, but do I believe it? Inscribing mad solutions to enigmas too close to be seen. What's clear is that I love you and could die of it—maybe all the stronger in that I'm no longer anything to you. *Tu m'obsèdes.* The mind reels. Let me see you again once, twice, or seven, or twelve times, no more, please, normally, if only to be rid of your phantom. We were both too terribly impatient. My mistake's always been in committing suicide on the eve of a revelation. Certainly there's an antidote against the poison you write of; could it be friendship? Could it? Could I learn to loathe you?

You used to miss me when I went to the bathroom. I'd based my life on such myths of charm. Now it's sickening to watch weeks go by without the relief of change. A month ago I stopped living. One word from you (which will never come) and I'd start all over. It's not your fault if you no longer love: it's the one thing we don't regulate. Yes, yes, from the beginning you glimpsed unnatural lights, why did you lead me on, slaughtering? Why did you lose faith? Oh, such holding back when I make these reproaches: you too must have unanswered questions. The irony is that so recently I was saying: "Finally, happiness, I've got it!" No sooner said than gone.

After strong pain could one end up loving again the person who caused it? *Réchauffer la soupe?* Before seeing that person one plays the martyr through inventions of memory. Suffering of which we ourselves are the cause is harder to conceive; conversely, inflicted on us, it becomes all we know. What's pathetic is that the end of unbalanced love (what love's balanced?) is the sole situation we can't control. Less than war. When I think of all the hearts I've hurt! Yet now have nothing more to look forward to—anticipation being the very nourishment of life. Oh God Claude, Oh God Claude, *je m'étouffe!*

This journal's always reflected reactions without giving reasons for them. My bed, only, has become a white wound licking me into itself. Art, the genius of choice, obliges selfishness. Joy, the art of resignation, pale, unselfish. You never indulged my "faults" (though I promised to repair them) and falsely accused me of atrocious motives.

Thanks to David Diamond, who had introduced us a week ago at the Scala restaurant, last night I visited Mitropoulos. Arriving at his bachelor quarters in the Great Northern at nine, a bundle of scores humbly under my arm, instantly I sensed his goodness, his open warmth, his resignation. We sat down to tea and honey. Ten minutes later I could no longer control the formalities and broke into tears. Mitropoulos closed the music he was examining, and asked me (why?) if I were being blackmailed. I began the story which flowed out like time and the river. He said look, let's forget the music for tonight and I'll take you to supper at The Blue Ribbon. Two hours later he said, as we sat over our empty cups of kirsch, looking straight at me, at the state I was in: "How I envy you! How I'd love to crawl, on the floor, in the mud, at the feet of one I loved. If you're strong you can rise from it all reborn, a new man with solider values.

But I'm too old now!" And we walked back to his hotel through the warm March wind as he told me stories of his youth. Those words, his more than gentle force and beauty, were like an icy balm for the moment at midnight. But all melted again this morning.

On the phone across the ocean you advised patience. Patience, my God! Obviously there's a difference between a little patience and the paranoid hell of waiting, waiting. I swear, that phone call will be my last abject action. No, it's dumb to swear such things. But I'll make a monstrous daily effort because I want your esteem as much as your love. As proof of goodwill, I've already stopped drinking. Almost. I'd say even it's . . . well . . . licked, and I'm a little scared, because not drinking is like not masturbating: explosion lurks. (Can explosions lurk?)

It's the first morning of spring and I wish I were dead. Got up at noon to see a sticky sky and one season leaking into the next as though the earth had stopped in its tracks, as though the hate and veneration which ooze into love were an eternal repetition of those tears which won't stop flowing, not to purify, but to insult the mud. Oh, I'll get over it! Meanwhile nights are sleepless or if I drop off it's to a recurrent dream in which you take me back, and I'm filled with joy, and wake up to the hard truth that everything's over and done, done, done, and the day's started hopelessly like yesterday, like last week and the week before. Sexual tension's been horrible: there may be pleasure with others, but they don't exist when I think of what I liked from you, and you in me, and I catch fire and can't put it out. Are any two people alike? Your New York humiliation was beyond control: far from your milieu you functioned only as my friend. In Holland we were in the same anonymous boat away from daily responsibility, but we'll never be again because we like our work. Don't we? When one person's on vacation and the other not, sparks fly unless there's a compromise. You were by defini-

tion in a *situation fausse*, and what could I do? Discretion now
seems everything, now that it's too late. I'd even prefer that no
one ever see us, that we meet in secret. I don't know what I'd
prefer, I'm thinking out loud, where, where did I go wrong? To
need you so much sometimes I could die, and dead could wait!

One afternoon you offered as sedative to poor B. (who still
bemoans his unrequited loves) the idea that a thing desired,
once had, loses its interest. That concept's more typical of
Americans than of French: the latter are less quick on the trigger
of novelty, stick closer to one circle of friends, dig deeper rather
than adding layers. The spineless man (I say it rationally) is one
who refuses the responsibility of a relationship, who accepts the
dessert without the spinach (to coin a phrase); the most de-
ranged drag-queen is more valid because more honest. Your
attitude of "I don't want to help you nor you to help me" is
nonetheless more French than American: during a century
France has known how to accept defeat, eyes closed to her
wounded pride. You'll say I'm far from the truth, that all these
arguments have nothing to do with you, that you're quite simply
sick of the whole bloody business. Jesus! Me too. Sick of self-
pity, but I'm talking from limbo solely with the hope of deliver-
ance. And so. I mean you meant to conquer first, love later. No,
Claude, I don't mean that, forgive me. You've got to have
strength to construct a working liaison without getting confined
to middle-classness which tempts you, I think, as much as me—
which frightens us. (That awful word "us.") You have pre-
conceived ideas (who doesn't?) and loved (idealized) me before
knowing me. My ideas are postconceived, I loved you for yourself. An *ideal* should not apply to an idea which changes
constantly.

Yes, in New York I knew everyone, you knew only me and
the need to get used to dozens of new circumstances in so short a
time. I mustn't defend myself too much or we'll never be on
equal terms. To be able to say: music must always come first!
But I read and reread your letters, between the lines, a thousand

new meanings. To have been so blind! and today clearly see those many moments you tried to escape at intermissions. How I understand your impatience to quit the bad dream of New York where you smothered like a kitten beneath a sow. Now it's I smothering, but don't need to kill myself. You've done it.

The lover renounced becomes a bore because he no longer functions as human. With the death rattle of any affair, they say, there's always one hurt more than the other. I love you, joylessly. Oh, still to write you dreams of vacations, tell you what I'm doing, ask the same of you, sexy letters! But this shock made life mechanical. I'd so love to have the word which would inspire me to go buy a ticket for Paris, a word saying: let's at least try to mend this mess enough for the remembrance to be nostalgic and not sordid, enough for us to see each other as friends and not monsters.

Should I admit what I did? Two years ago I met a baker named Marcel on the Avenue Friedland. He specialized in pastries to my delight, then to my disgust explained how filthy his work was: peach pies covered by smoke and saliva. Anyway, we got better acquainted in a hallway, and saw each other maybe twice later, and then I stood him up, and that was that. Well, two weeks ago in fierce loneliness I sent a letter, a love letter, to *Marcel le pâtissier* with no last name on the street without numbers where he once lived. The letter was returned: Address Unknown. . . . In *Other Voices, Other Rooms* there's a character in love who no longer knows where his lover is. He writes the world over, care of General Delivery—to Oran, Frisco, Shanghai, Frankfurt, in vain. He hadn't got it through his head that the incident was one-sided, that it was finished, that his friend no longer cared. Today I'm that character, nor do I know where you are, nor have I got it through my head that you don't care, but continue to hope against hope and pray on my knees for all soon to be better between us. The worst moment of a life is when you look in the mirror and say (knowing it to be true): "No one wants you anymore."

I think more about you in not having you than when I did,
my cloud, my steed, javelin, sapphire. I've never loved anyone
but you—the others were . . . And I'll love you always. . . .
We endow our poor lovers with godly traits, then destroy them
for being mortal. Make one repugnant gesture that would permit
me to despise you, a release from this tender anguish which I
stalk, stroking the brief past with its thorns and afternoons at the
Pont Mirabeau or the Buttes Rouges, and the first evening when
I sang you my songs, which you pretended to like. Love with its
soggy crust and petulance must come before the music it's now
hard to hear because I ruminate too much, too much on you
until there's melting in tears six times a day. Yet what can save
me, bring me through the universal intestines—music staves
which resemble bars—if not the sounds I'm supposed by God to
write?

How far France seems! Her smells and rivers and nights and
streets. To return for a long stay! It's not a question of money or
desire, but I won't go back until I can honestly admit it's not an
attempt to reactivate a union (dead on one side) whose recall
will always be the most precious of my life. Half of that life's
already lived and I can count on the fingers of one hand the
number of months I've known peace. Is it worth the trouble to
languish over someone five thousand kilometers away who
doesn't give a damn? Am I not another person than the one who
wrote that giant letter from the boat in December a century ago?
A century ago, when a green world seemed to open where
tonight there is only a void. You dropped a bomb without
turning to see the explosion, leaving me to limp through the
ruins. But maybe he who's left is the more powerful—he held
on. But the cause, the causes! You tell me that the mass of
contradictions are contradictions only to me. Well, sure! And
so?

I won't rest until they're swept up. Was it conflict of careers or
a jealous disdain of my hamminess that got on your nerves? But
I don't want your slavery—except to my body from time to time.

Why on earth write all this? Nothing but an insignificant wind, a sentimental breath which sounded feebly in an immense Sahara, heard by no one, by nothing except a heart that drips, loves, bleeds, snaps, wants still to give itself away. You sought yourself in me but found nothing.

Today's your birthday. Is it possible to dwell on you more intensely than I've done for the third of a year? Not a minute goes without wondering where you are and who you're seeing. It's classic—the banal fixations of leftover people. But one mustn't, at such moments, expect consideration from anywhere. Nor is there consolation in thinking back to our frequent conversations which remain my most valuable possessions. Your image persists like my love, my love and dreams vomit up a thousand pardons from which I awake each day with a face drenched in tears.

You left America a month ago, and since then there's been not one gentle word from you. If you could have foreseen the aftermath, would you have tempered your revenge? No. By accusing me of irony do you clear a bad conscience? But letting myself destroy myself is a sin. Was I too weak or too strong for you? Could you tolerate such fishwifely questions? You make me dance to a whip of icicles yet won't listen to the musical shrieks I can no longer notate, notation which no longer makes a difference, the difference in your future loves will be lukewarm, but at least you'll never be the same again.

The weather's still marvelous this morning, sweet and silvery, bringing a terrific urge to make love, not done (or hardly, or badly) since you went away. With whom? The bizarre mixture of my talent and physique loathed or envied has never brought much more than sadness. Everyone thinks my narcissism is unequaled. *C'est faux.* I'm less sure than most, but openly admit what others hide like gangrene, and it's a fact I've been more loved than I've loved. To love is to put on the spot, whereas I take what I see and make it mine.

Love, which fascinates a lover, is tedium to nonparticipants. In the act of love I see myself less . . . *comment dirai-je?* . . . like a child simultaneously tortured and protected. It's not perilous. Nothing's more perilous than reproaches: the act reproached is, five minutes later, far in the past, and people alter. I'm capable of visible motions of the heart; yours are invisible, therefore stronger. A blindman knows how to garnish his dream. I've gone too far to pull out now. I never forget a thing.

Do you know what it's like to wait? Are you able to be unhappy? (Love's just a habit, only a habit.) Does loneliness never seem sad to you? (They tell me I was an eleven-month baby.) Can you ever be jealous? (I've asked you seven and a half times.) You're in my life but I am not in yours.

I love you. Because you don't see as I see, you miss everything. But if you saw as I saw I wouldn't love you, for I need only mysteries. Music is a mystery. To *understand* music is to love it less. (I love it less and less.) Nor do you know much about me. It's better that way. I want to be *the* person for you, meaning the one thing beyond your work you need. Thus I could spend years away from you. Yet alone my successes would be empty: they need to be shared.

You dissimulate all emotions—which gives your face a stingy beauty. If my principal quality (quality, not virtue) is frankness, yours is concentration; you never lose a minute. Thus all your minutes are lost. Though maybe nothing's lost. Or gained. No love is happy. Art is happy, though life is drab. An only son is a child in a tower who, when he becomes a man, holds onto his independence as to his mother, that is, to something inexistent. . . . A free man? Free of what? For solitude does not exist either.

I show my foliage too much, heart, ruses, I shouldn't: I'm the mountain who goes to Mohammed. But no one changes anyone.

Since no one has anyone, how do other people pass the time? Love is impossible. But when it becomes possible it's no longer love.

Thinking incessantly on you, you infiltrate yourself like a jiggly flame between myself and the music staves. At heart I'm a good person; one's never credulous enough—not the French. My passivity is active.

To a point of sickness you're obsessed with freedom. But, I repeat, freedom from what? Liberty's just an easier path, and you'll find out one day too late. Love's a specific renunciation you ignore—a race in a labyrinth, and only young love lasts. One must descend, descend to the chest's roots, a hard trip for two. You travel the world without really leaving home, without investigating foreign manners, elbowing true feelings which make you shiver though you cross an ocean to see the one you maintain you admire. But you remain a tourist too in love. You made me crawl, the easier to despise me, and despised me, the easier to rid yourself. So doing, you've grown to a giant, are all I cherish, block the way to new experiences, to work, and won't disappear. *Claude? Claude? Tu m'écoutes?* Our recent *rapports* now seem as strange as a detective novel made by an illogical poet, so I contradict myself (a privilege of fluid souls), though not in the essential of what was named Charity that day we rode over Washington bridge in Morris' car. If I praise myself it's self-defense. Because you've cut off my feet, then laugh when I limp—buried me deep and ask why I stifle.

All this is no more than the blurred angle of a dull story you'd prefer flinging to silence. Such arguments could no more interest you than your ability to see through my eyes as I see you—like divinity and ghoul. I observe my errors. Don't you prefer someone soft whom you can, without complication, dominate. Are you "my type"? What's a type? Did you take for vanity what was enthusiasm? Do you have my number? Speak my language? Dig my camp? No. You don't realize that, like you, I'm French, and though the French might wittily be true to speech, they never, like Americans, boringly speak the truth. To speak the truth is to speak one-dimensionally.

I'll keep these sinister gifts in my red red heart until they mix with my blood through the dissolution of sweet events in a future as uncertain as your feelings for me, but no, no, what's the use, I give up, give in, surrender. Thrown to the ground I'd paw it, but no longer have the strength to say *au revoir* or *adieu*, because I can't stand anything anymore. A venture on which two beings mutually embark—if it must end, must end mutually. But that's easier said than done. Let me now take my will in two hands and rebecome myself without you.

We see among the perfume bottles, plants and bedclothes, a murdered woman's head; but where now is the decapitator roaming, what thinking? Or we see sparrows lying in the snow, fallen from their sleepy perch when the young adventurer with a thoughtful sword slashed off their legs; but does he linger to observe the agony? Or through a keyhole we watch the doctor gaze into a twitching orifice recently disturbed by some rugged phallus whose carrier is today far off (while the victim stays in the office). Victim? . . . The tree was grounded by the hunter come and gone. The girl's heart's broken by the now-invisible lover because present is immediately past. Who, what, where are *these* hours, those all-powerful ones, walking, who couldn't remain to consider the sexy suffering? We see the kisser and kissed and though the kiss can't be undone the kisser will run off not knowing because not caring the same way. We see those tenacious kissed ones lament the ever-changing replacements, wishing like the mad the present were fixed and that they in their turn could have ripped off the live bludgeons of their thoughtless divine assassins and kept them to own always in an attic of mementos . . . You long to be free. And everything living wants to live (does an orchid try suicide?). Yet the new convict can't wait to see his future home. Yes, all long for freedom; necks of shepherds and sailors strain against T-shirts and wind.

You're indefatigable because you economize the efforts of your heart. You will say: "What a beautiful picture," but not that Mary Magdalene was *amoureuse*. You appreciate a *chef-d'oeuvre* more than the heart that made it. That strength is in lack of reaction; those who don't react are dead. People passionate about the arts are heartless: green oils and high strings come before "real life." Yes, you do react, but it's so rare that the glow in your eyes is that of an unknown planet which I catch and freeze and hide away in a private treasure chest. Perhaps only artists (so-called) can afford the luxury of love or madness which empties and fills them, a lonely luxury by definition. I only like what I can't understand. But all masterpieces are a bit boring; it's hard to catch on quickly to new rhythms. You are a bit boring.

I have been too much loved, which has led me too much to drink. Truth to tell I'm shy with people. And animals. I drink only for the hangover from which emerges the moment of truth, the *coup de grâce*, the involuntary detail, the All of engrossment underlining laughter of human hyena females on a subway. Trees, porpoises, don't bother to laugh—or are they always? It's not that they don't give a damn: they don't *not* give a damn. There's a demon in sobriety causing wars that could be avoided if the sober realized they're really lushes who don't know it. Unfortunately most people aren't drunk most of the time. It helps in meeting people, a hangover, by its power for concentration: concentration toward a spot on the ceiling which eventually moves (it always *did,* but we never waited long enough in bed). When our ears ring do we listen? When the larks flap before our very eyes who sees them? . . . Hangovers make you receptive, hot and hungry. A stupor of illness permits focus on a thumbtack generating light of its own, a luminous jewel and our sole gift to the unknown. There's a fourth dimension to the hungover world through which we perceive the fifth-dimensional one of sobriety. Another is sobriety's prisoner with only three auras.

How *do* people meet? There's a look of possible love exchanged by strangers (at a party, on a bus) who, through shyness or duty, never speak—and spend their remaining lives regretting the fact. Sometimes I feel the most faithful union is that sealed by a glance from a passing train to a boy in a pear tree.

Your systematic and somewhat inhuman way of seeing everything could end up exasperating me, making me so ill with jealousy I'd roll in your old sheets, bury my head in that drawer of soiled clothes like a bee in gray roses eager to retrieve your crotch and underarms, needing to possess your yesterday's sweat. An envy of shoes for being closer than I to you. An itch to crawl under the sleeping eyelids so that no dream could waft you where I was uninvited. Now I cannot think of any of those others without crying, and I think of them always. But this time I'm not going to cry, not this time, oh no!

You compartmentalize emotions as you do teeth. You are not made to comprehend artists whose "curious" lives have always been my daily bread. But you comprehend other things which will reunite us.

Today an envelope from Pavia encloses the despair of P. Which leaves me indifferent. See how the years pass? How now I am groaning for you who seem to need nothing? Or do you? Don't tell me. Insistence leads to lies. Don't judge America through me. Drinking again helps remembrance of things past, though will permit scant recall of what's now occurring.

Always injure the perfect in a flash, then choke on your own sweet time, the virtues of idleness. (Play hard to get in haste, repent in leisure.)

What on earth can you this afternoon be thinking there in France? A glance would show you my change of heart if you'd look here just once more. No, having failed to demolish you some of me died instead, the part that alone you could retain: your notion of me. Can we hurry to make new friends and be reborn in their ideas? But what of those I've never known who, from a distance have seen and loved me—and who have died? Did I feel, far off, that piece of myself which they possessed, also disappear?

What an ugly sunset!

Yes, we act according to our dreams. Let's act according to our real needs and not have wars. Dreamer, I built from something real (our meeting) something unreal (your devotion), but since public opinion sways you, you strangle me at the very moment I cry out: *je t'aime!* Happiness is the perfect balance between work and love. But balance is stupid, and happiness should be aimed at only secondarily. Can you dream, you? Have you recognized yourself in any of these words? You bastard?

This is a love letter—the last of so many. Never sent. After such vows, with a desire to rediscover myself and be alive again, I look continually over my shoulder nevertheless and understand nothing. So, seeking librettos, I read *Camino Real* and immediately see:

"The little comfort of love?"

"Is that comfort so little?"

"Caged birds accept each other but flight is what they long for."

For myself I dream of being tied down. But can any self-made oath truly help us change? How can we keep from being invaded by a sort of hazy sorrow at the futility of any try at loving? Finally love becomes only a frail scabrous game; and if, proudly, you show your tactics too much, you've lost before you've started. I don't know why you suggest that out of bed I may show no real interest in you, but you're not the first to say this. That bed, that wound, and I recall my long years of lying there inert and alive with a hangover late into the warm wet spring afternoons of darkness with curtains slightly blowing, and from the outside world came the far sound of separated children laughing or hammering, or the ting-a-ling of a Good Humor cart. You were then not yet in my life, and today I am no longer in yours though not two months ago you came over a toy sky to find me. And I'd even thought of suicide to clear up the mess. But one can see. Suicides which work, fail: having your cake and not eating, or something. So I try to be persuaded that music must always come first (will always be the one faithful love), and that creation is the genius of inevitable choice and elimination and seeing things as they are not. Thus seen, they become, since all exists. Literally I'm dressed in the skins of former love. And a lover is the worst rival since there is another ego to feed.

Nobody, even if he's fed up, has the right to do to another what you've done, in changing without warning, condemning without trial. Yet haven't I done it myself so many times? You claim you're the least complex of beings, and it's true for you who've never tried to know yourself as I have tried to know you. At such moments we find reproval or seek consolation in any breeze, and I came across a Whitman verse of unrequited love and set it last night to notes. . . . The headsman locks the dungeon and goes off forever calmly. Put an ocean between you and the prisoner and you've no more worries. Unless the prisoner escapes.

Love is mutual respect; I'd forgotten that you existed too. And love is always a game. And an invention. And what we learned in the last affair trains us what to unlearn in the next; yet when the next's over we realize that what we now refrained from was just what should have been done.

You helped me look into myself, so I love you, to know how to live this little life, and also, curiously because you didn't encourage me to love you. I love you for what you are not, with a constructive ego, the best way: one can't healthily love without faith in oneself; and though I haven't it anymore, it will come back.

April 1st. *Poisson d'avril!* Have lost nearly all the false narcissism which was nevertheless a refuge for one who lacked a base of self-assurance in spite of appearances. If I could replace it with faith! Only we know such good resolutions aren't easily realized. These kind warm days of early spring I perceive through a fog seeping down my throat that makes me cough up dumb old things to be thrown at new ears.

Today if by chance you were to come across these pages you'd hate me in not finding yourself because you don't see yourself as I do yet you think you see yourself entirely. Never again will I believe what were nevertheless the dearest words I've ever heard—those murmured by you in discovering yourself *grâce à moi.* Pray God that if ever I'm granted another love it'll be on another plan or plane, because one can't ripen by always following (as one evening we longly followed your Canal Saint Martin) experience after experience in exactly the same fashion, unassured and possessive epoch after epoch. But this future love: could it be again with you? Even though you've withdrawn and taken back all you gave? Even though you've cultivated my soul while deriding my family? Even though we're new children about to inscribe on the erased blackboard? Even if I've started again to drink like a fish in former routines? Even when you deny old desires while the whole autumn through you struggled with me against an innate laziness (even to the point of wanting to do a libretto), and regretted only that you weren't the first of my loves (although you *were*—and I can't stop harboring that)? Even if you knew that now I stuff myself with sleeping pills (which used to appall me) in order to forget you a few hours a day? And even if you knew that I roam around each night looking for just anyone to fill the wounded bed which seems all the same to stay empty, empty, empty, empty? As long as you're sure of me this will be impossible. But the neurotic me (*le moi nevrosé*) of whom you once were sure, he exists no more. How I loathe you.

How I love you. Face growing gaunt and lips tight. Handsome does as handsome is. This is brought home so strongly now when entering a bar, and no head turns. Does a tiger consider the antelope's pain? or an Iroquois administer anesthetic before scalping? Suddenly today I am standing apart to see the young among themselves, their arms frailer than spider strands and voices like spider breath failing. But what unrehearsed voices! what strong, strong arms! Old songs, their skin, the tears, the expressionless, the isolating, the young among themselves. I used to think that being conscious of your own youth was a first sign of age. Nevertheless, the young, with all their teasy ways, *do* have smoother skin and see their whole lives before them. Or minutes. But minutes are life, and what can I look forward to but years?

Yes, now I can see the years and how the past drags like a peacock's tail ever longer which yet erects a luminous fan blowing and hiding and sweeping the traces and helping what might come. How exclusive they get!—or rather, they've no need of exclusion. (Where now are all those who once said they loved me?) I can stand off to see—how clearly? For to children together age grows invisible, no outside exists. Through mists the world interprets, forcing wars upon them with bad senility ruling. Yet to whom the fault? Age, or rather decrepitude, is boredom of body; it's not that we're no longer able, just that we're sick and tired of putting the same old carcass to the same old uses. But while the seasons unquestionably repeat themselves we go to pot. . . . Enough is too much. Still, a little too much is just enough for me. I yen for you whose musk inebriates across the ocean. Who can add more than bromides to the universal

plot? Children enamored are self-sufficient, blind to repetition of
fault after fault. Age, the world, plots (having no more to do);
and what can it comprehend—except through remembrance—of
young love occurring far from time? Far from space, love young,
love young, for whom even force of wind or smell of sweat is
new, all new, learning what I've forgotten, remaining alive when
I'm dead, who (being born each minute) breathe more and more
the oxygen I've less and less of.

For me there are no more first times. But at least the Lovelies
of our cinema have more in common with me than with Poppea
—or even Lillian Russell—for the simple reason that we're all
living now. And whether or not the Lovelies like it, they and I
will forever breathe parallel lives. That's one consolation. Except
for me, can the naughty old world pretend to give a damn (since
it does give terrible damns), spinning, trapping, recoiling, con-
spiring, leading them to misfire? How *not* be consoled in knowing they'll finally die! Dear one, everything dies, even our
children, even the sun.

Today I received this letter:

DEAR MR. ROREM,
    Your frankness, and urge for outburst and exhibit of
your distress is exactly the most important element a creator, a composer must have besides his knowledge. That is
why your music spoke to my feelings and that is why I
programmed it for the evening of 12 October 57. That is
for your information, and as a kind of antidote against
your actual poisoned condition. May thus, the power of a
spiritual sperma annihilate the power of another wasted
one!!
    With many friendly feelings
                                    DIMITRI MITROPOULOS

Do you recall, in that Amsterdam hotel, the plump Negro girl
whose window gave onto our courtyard, and on whom we spied

at midnight as she, naked, fingered a silent keyboard with two dictionaries on her head? . . . But where is a homeland when you've stayed away as long as I? America always seems home while away and a return is as inviting as the renewal of an old love affair. But being here, I haven't yet really *seen* New York, not knowing where I am now, nor how to take hold, nor the way to truly love myself, which would help me learn to love you. These many French pages indicate this, for I criticize you at being incapable of an "errand into the maze" and speak of the wounded bed as though it were a title. But have we a right to accuse others of failing at things we ourselves don't dare? Today is gray and hot with a lacy rain, and we're well into April.

How little nations understand each other, or try. That's said from the impotent placement of a poet who's spent a good part of his life liking an earth he's not understood. In Paris, an uprooted American, he was held secure by the balance imposed on a false shelter by two powers like winds battling. And learned never to expect anything from anyone except himself. Now he feels the start of a wavering. Which way? When, if ever, we see each other again, we'll be the same actors but in a new play.

After midnight. Weather's turned cold. Back from the movies, the movies where you always liked most to look at me—in profile with glasses. How I adored being alone with you! Never take a Frenchman literally: promises are no more than exercises in style. It's not for you I say it: you with a chest frozen before the prospects of a marriage which would have comprised so many readjustments. So you returned to a rich solitude. Where now are you going? who frequenting? what indeed was your former way? . . . Was I perhaps less capable than you of holding the reins of that heart-shaped horse, but don't realize it since you in detesting me make me want you all the more? From the start we'd both based the whole thing wrong: you on vanquished fantasy, me on unmysterious possession, whereupon I lowered myself into a disguise as an owl showing shallowest sides (saving the good ones for work). Rejection without advice.

To live is to make souvenirs, both in romance-memories and those left through solitary production. To love is to desire to live *with*, and is more than only life. Without it there is no reason, though reasons *for* it have no definition. Sterile today and tomorrow I'm making no memories. Have I an unrequited love for myself? "You're beautiful." "So are you." "Well shall we come together and make something ugly? Thereby producing from two negatives a positive."

There can be he who kills himself at the death of a loved one *not* so as to retrieve the lover in heaven, but so the two can be in the same position in relation to the world.

Later is too late.

To say: I love you. Look. A perfectly lovely sentiment. Those words speak louder than actions though I don't know it yet, for knowing would mean I'm no longer young. Of course thoughts sound louder than words even if, alas, we only grow old above the waist. To think: just two days ago I was always the youngest at parties.

Well, that's how love is—don't we agree? Clenched heart, a parade of good-byes, then the long good-bye, a long postscript, an expedition of waiting. I remember the muse of love growing larger as she walked away with no cure for our sentiment trailing like a sick rat on a leash. But the impossibility makes love love, whose only clinching vow (we all agree) is dying. The desire fulfilled to be indispensable turns out duller than the disciplines of art. Oh, that dumb need to share . . . Here lie I, caressing my thigh, and calmly file and clip and trim and smooth the ends of my chewed hands, lying demurely with lowered eyes in the midst of our vertiginous galaxy, for comfort offering order to the sky that doesn't know that it doesn't know. What goes wrong with chaos that we must classify? Must invent also a trap for the heart (I, for one, always fall in), hoping permanence squashes solitude. *Such* a habit! Yet try to retrieve it and find that now old lovers have new lives too (or has anyone anyone but himself?): that mysterious surprise makes us love them all the more. Absence, it's agreed, stimulates fancy. Wait, wait, and wait— kill, kill, and kill. Oh, I love you . . . But when the door's finally knocked, *how* to react! Open-armed?

Depuis que vous avez quitté New York . . . since you left New York you've not unhappily left me but settled like lead even when I come home late on purpose from hollow exploits, torso gnarled as a cauliflower and nape bruised by strangers' teeth. You, though, smashed the heart into gelatin unable to harden toward new adventures as I stagger blinded among grimaces. The *cafard* is insistent, ever present, like a sentimental poison numbing. I feel I've no longer any power over anyone. Your letters which envied the joy I may have known previous to knowing you, which promised relief, now burn these fingers which begin to find a joy owed to nothing but self-inquest. I'm destined to live with myself so must get used to it. Later's too late, and you were too strong. Happiness may exist only in sharing and lovers have a marvelous solitude *à deux*. But it's also a selfishness *à deux*. How boring are loving couples to their friends! bereft of elegance or dignity! Whenever a friend gets married we lose him. How stupid the happy lover! and how stupid the rejected one! Fickle as fairies who break each other's hearts more easily than peasants twist geese necks . . . You must never learn how indispensable, irreplaceable you've become, how I seek you in nightmares, and by day pitifully in the features of others, in wet places, bars somber and stuffed, or rainy streets or public baths, bottles of gin, or slimy mouths offered risibly. You resent what I've been able to keep of you in me, the you of yesterday who is no more and whom you've forgotten.

The sad thing is that we were both so weak, so dumbly weak after such wasted investments. Anyone's capable of 90 percent more than he does, but only inertia keeps us going. This evening I'm so depressed in remembering all the failures of my demi-life, in knowing suicide solves nothing since we won't hear the aftermaths. With all my heart I wanted this to work. It's the disappointment of a life.

Oh those I've loved and never seen who've inhabited my body, shouted through my lips, or sometimes cried, all those. And our stylish books on love as a sharing bit: they presuppose mutuality so never propose solutions to the unrequited. If I wrote songs the choicest verses would be those weeping down from latrine walls.

For days you don't leave my mind. That smile hurts, the smile pains for weeks, a star pressed on the brains. I carry it everywhere like a briefcase from city to city. You can board a plane, you know, in Stockholm with a hangover, and land a few hours later in Casablanca—with the same hangover. Or the same banged-up heart or slaphappy smile—what's the difference! I've done it. But hurt does die. Things do, you know. Or do you? A force of love builds prisons: in memory of a nightmare. Or maybe the nightmare is just its being over.

Love is a fantasy and no one's fantastic anymore. Shall I invent a fantasy for you? Listen. Since Youth is Body, that's what initially attracts. One step beyond creates a really physical romance. If the outside delights us, how much more gorgeous is the interior's clockwork of artery and purple nerves, its maze of muscle and yellow organs! Let's take a doctor as hero, since he (not a dentist or Jack the Ripper) normally explores the corridors around our bones; he, and only he, sees past the silly beauty of a face, can slash open his mistress' belly confronting all color, construction, and patient evolutionary threads. When alone he longs for the sight of his lady's lungs, the touch of her real heart, her cold odor of blood through a honeycomb-skeleton. He hears her veins and would lick her spine. . . . It began when an unprepossessing woman entered the office of my surgeon, who

ignored her face and chest and tiresome complaints, but the
instant of incision smashed heaven's doors: never has he known
such a velvet liver whose cancer flows golden. With unbounded
affection he weeps into her wound. . . . But she heals and goes
off. He grows lonely, sentimental for that distant orderly inner
room. Can his nostalgia prepare a trap into which she'll tumble
and break her stitches, bringing her back exposed to his arms
which will caress again the long pink warmth of her intestines?

Mitropoulos is right: remarkable health can result from abject
dejection, and from rejection wherein one is nothing, nothing.
Yet what's the use of being healthy in a sick society? I miss you
as one of my own members which however I myself tore off in
trying to understand, like children rip open their dolls. To
penetrate and receive in giving and taking through these two
acts (which are really one) is to love. Each note of music is
written for you, whether you will or no, so strong is the need to
give, to give; and I need you because I love you, though I don't
love you because I need you. I hope. Why not marry? You can't
live amongst the willows and wasps as though they were your
neighbors: man, dreadful as he is, is all we've got. Don't keep
yourself from it.

I really liked being in your company. With P. in the old days
I always felt: "Go away, so that I can see us in relief." With you
it's: "Come back, because I can no longer stand to think." But
you're far off, and will stay far off. That first evening, you said:
"The sad thing is that Americans must eventually go away."
Later we concocted a love without identity.

During the past two months and for perhaps two months I'll
have gone from shock to paralysis to astonishment to rage to
despair to *l'anéantissement* to uncertainty to resignation to selfishness to indifference to remembrance to forgetfulness. I don't
wish you to be my life, but to be part of it, to help me again to
hear the sounds of nature. These ears have grown numb in

trying to become your equal. When we first met the days were growing shorter, colder. Now they're lengthening into spring-time and it's possible that soon I'll return to Paris. To be acquainted with all the seasons in you so as to better analyze the source of this failure, to better feel Ives' music named "The Unanswered Question!"

For weeks in the middle of the night I've burdened the saintly Morris Golde, wept and pleaded for advice as for a drug. With endless patience he calms, suggests, tolerates, comprehends, lends his time as I crumble, and aids genuinely. Next day another shot is required. But I'll be forever grateful.

We failed thanks to the twentieth century. Because one flies over seas. Because one's in a hurry. Because so many of us see love as being loved (and we're right) that few are left over. Because of the difference between falling and staying in love, because we confuse relief-from-loneliness with infatuation. Loneliness is hard work, infatuation is laziness. Not just anyone can be unhappy—*n'est pas solitaire qui veut*. Laziness takes us away from the *practice* of love, like practice of music or dentistry. We're certain of only the past and death. *Et encore!* We're ashamed of love though it's the cheapest remedy for solitude. Or is love evil because it destroys the necessity of aloneness? Art's a substitute for love, but paradoxically on a higher plane.

Having read and drunk everything, what's left but you? Still, we threw ourselves into a disintegrated fusion where, once bars were down, we were quickly without the miracle of astonish-ment at those discoveries which must constantly renew them-selves, that two become one yet stay two. Is love the act of giving without sacrificing? Even in receiving one gives in sex they say. Bromides of responsibility, respect, love is the offspring of lib-erty, the do-it-yourself banalities of Erich Fromm, who has recipes for every kind of love except the unrequited. (My self-love is unrequited!) But respect is hard without knowledge, and we're unknowable even to ourselves. I had desired, Claude, that you relinquish your secret in making you suffer rather than in liking you.

It's very late at night and I'm back from the Tourel recital with Jean Stein. Over the weekend I was drunk to obliteration, which somehow cleansed me nevertheless, awakening early in the headache haze to look closely and in a single dimension at my blanket of red and orange which became *childhood colors seen again for the first time.* Only a hangover can reproduce such a focus.

Have always felt a little guilty at liking what pleases me. From that comes excitation for music, pastries, and for certain acts of love. And from that comes the sadistic fear, alcoholic.

The courage of upset starts to evaporate thank God and I don't much want happiness but vital activity. A dentist plays God by fabricating a true part of a human body which his customers will carry around until death and long after. A composer can't say as much. Not to be able to love doesn't necessarily imply not to be able to love Ned Rorem—though you'd never believe it after all this. Nevertheless, disenchanted, you couldn't prepare me for the downfall. In *The Robbers* I have the Novice say: "There is a difference between the planning and the act." Can false love (oh my) be so fast substituted for true, as you maintain, without infection having germinated from the start? We never calmly asked where are we going? have we tried to keep first impressions which are finally all that count?

Failed thanks to the century . . . The French fright of being caught by feelings. Everything's now more hurried than basics, we've no longer time for anything. Americans are cured through excess, the French through ridicule. Modern life, alas, is no longer adapted to the Tragic. To perfumed wounds. Ridicule? An American's ridicule would be to go back to Paris and find you once again involved with a phantom. *Mais il faut être capable de tout.*

Am I going mad? Unfortunately not. Insanity means being unaware of insanity.

Drinking too much again without question. Between two binges, float foggily to the surface and learn that finally I've been granted a Guggenheim. I'm gladder for my family than for me. But it will be a living for another year or two, and that, plus the inclusion of my works on programs of both Ormandy and Mitropoulos for next season, stabilizes somewhat these shuddering months. Now what do, where go this summer? Stay in America? That would surely be wisest. Until you've ripened and met yourself I cannot meet you. Or is it my business to love—the leisure to love—yours, to fix teeth? Maybe you're too young for me. But to deny me tenderness just because I request it seems perverse. . . . So much indecision these last two months! So many new loves signifying less than cricket tunes in other summers! So much clairvoyance when I thumb through this very diary of ten years ago!

Patience is a virtue of petty souls. Credulous as a child, I maintain trust despite contrary proofs of this fickle menacing world. The trust is painful and silly and valuable, I wish not to be cured. *Par cette foi je veux vivre et mourir*—sang Villon. And without it, how write music which no one will hear as I heard it?

Well, now I'll retire with a kiss on your forehead. (Don't recoil like that! Stop fearing what isn't!) *Ciào!*

It's not the unapproachable noncaring you that I like but the other so kind from yesterday gnawing my souvenirs like a fragrant cancer. If I could only retrieve that yesterday through you of tomorrow—for meanwhile my soul lacks entrances for creeping beauties, strangers all. Naturally it's stupid to go to

Knowing I go Thursday to Paris, and now is Monday, I've already left, yet still here. Time drags by at a snail's pace. More trying than an arrival too soon. Meanwhile I've not had a drink for two months, and roast myself all naked daily in the last sun, for the Île de France will be cold they say. I compose and onanize and read, liking my ~~third~~ third Symphony, the human body firm and fragile as a paper-clip.

Boris Kochno ~~has written~~ mailed from Switzerland a lovely letter to Marie Laure in which he speaks of himself in the third person as someone he met on a beach who asked after her — but he was unable to reply. And Felix Labisse has gone to Brazil after baptizing me (he's 50) as his ~~friend Jean Leuvrais~~ solves all these puzzles irrefutably: those he admires or loves he makes a part of his life whether they know it ~~or him~~ or not; he works the strings of people a hemisphere ~~away~~ away — their least decision has his approval. He's not bothered with the flesh.
News flash: Nature improves on art.

. . . . ⟵——————— asterisks

PARIS, early autumn 1957

Yes, I've come back to Paris two nights ago and have already had my homecoming cure of disgrace, ~~a~~ face a bit ~~shacked~~ hacked which comes (as we know) from the jerky shaving with a hangover. Cities, cities, cities as doll town mazes. My hand's still none too solid and the Paris air is heavy, cool, dark. I am blond, depressed, tan. If, like they say, I have

A page from this diary.

The writer of this diary at six months (Indiana, 1924).

Chicago, 1941   *(photo by Richard Jacob*

Paris, 1953
(photo by Guy Bourdin)

New York, 1957   *(photo by (*

Portrait by Larry Rivers, New York, 1958.

With Virginia Fleming, preparing for her recital
in Town Hall, New York, 1956. (*photo*, **N.Y. Times**)

Mattiwilda Dobbs also prepares for her Town Hall concert, 1956.
(*photo*, **N.Y. Times**)

Ellen Faull rehearses the solo in N.R.'s *Poets' Requiem* for Town Hall premiere conducted by Margaret Hillis in 1957. (*photo*, N.Y. Times)

Phyllis Curtin poses, before 1960 recital in Buffalo. (*photo*, Buffalo Courier-Express)

Marie Laure, la Vicomtesse
Noailles (*photo by Patrick O'Higg*

Dimitri Mitropoulos

Eugene Ormandy rehearses N.R.'s *Design* with the Philadelphia Orchestra, 1957. *(photo by Adrien Siegel)*

Josef Krips looks over N.R.'s score for *Eagles*, 1960. *(photo,* Buffalo Evening News*)*

EVOLUTION OF A SONG

First pencil draft

to Alice Esty and David Stimer

NIGHT CROW

Th. Roethke

Ned Rorem

Copy in india ink

to Alice Esty and David Stimer

NIGHT CROW

THEODORE ROETHKE

NED ROREM

Publication
(Edition Peters)

N.R.'s sister Rosemary, at Beloit College.

Morris Golde in Connecticut.
(*photo by Ted Tessler*)

Shirley Gabis Rhoads (Xénia) and her son Paul in Cuernavaca.

Joseph LeSueur in New York.

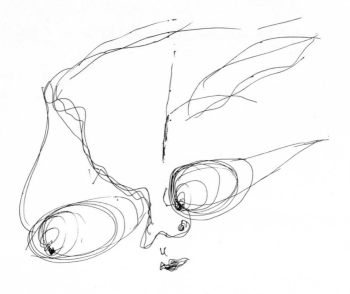

Drawings by N.R. while under mescalin in 1958.

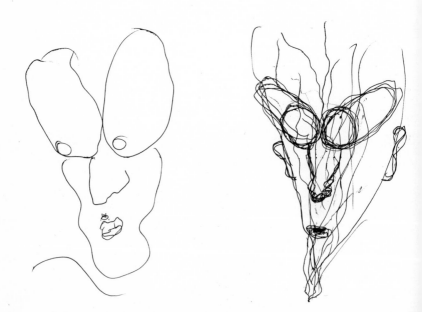

Benita Valenti, Wayne Conner and Dorothy Krebill in the TV version of N.R.'s opera, *A Childhood Miracle* (libretto by Elliott Stein), Philadelphia, 1956.

N.R. with composer Arthur Benjamin in London, 1955.

er Lyon, Oscar Dominguez, nette Lyon and N.R. in tume for the Bal du Port Hyères, September 1957.

THE UNIVERSITY OF BUFFALO

MUSIC DEPARTMENT

SLEE LECTURE-RECITALS
NED ROREM

COMPOSER
and
PERFORMANCE

WITH A PROGRAM
OF AMERICAN SONGS

performed by
REGINA SARFATY
MEZZO - SOPRANO

NED ROREM
PIANO

THURSDAY
DECEMBER 3, 1959
8:30 P.M.

ADMISSION FREE   BAIRD HALL

NG COVERS

by Reginald Pollack

by Kurt Seligmann

Alice B. Toklas and Eddie Waterman attend an all-Rorem concert at the
American Embassy in Paris. Among those behind them are Hélène de Wendl,
Sherband Sidéry, Madame de Lucinge, Paul Goodman, Jeanne Dubost,
Madame Seinkeiwitz, Jacques Dupont, Henri Sauguet, Rina Rosselli, Michel
Chauveton and Pierre Guérin.

by Charles-Henri Ford,
Rome, 1954

Photo by Eugene Cook,
New York, 1960

by Horst,
Oyster Bay, 1956

by Man Ray,
Paris, 1954

Virgil Thomson, N.R., William Flanagan and Phyllis Curtin rehearsing for the second *Music for the Voice by Americans* concert in 1960.

Maurice Abravanel, conductor of the Utah Symphony Orchestra, and N.R. iron out a few problems in the tone poem, *Lions,* 1966.
(*photo,* Salt Lake Tribune, Utah)

America and expect the Netherlands. What you French call liberty is really a type of discretion, which doesn't keep you from making mincemeat of foreigners' frankness. Our affair (problem) was never resolved (ended) in a fair (intelligent) fashion, which is why I so want to see (disdain) you again, and may buy a ticket to France (the past). Being unsure of yourself you broke off unfinished business. And yes, happiness is paid for. You knew it, paid. While I've been accusing myself too much, to your advantage, am now but a rag with eyes watching the gas stove. No longer accuse anyone. Your cowardice gives me force.

Happiness paid for? Yes, if you've not the nerve to sustain it free; if you can't resist rendering ugly the most touching notions; if you search for it instead of a rebirth through it. Happiness in itself is ineffectual, a fragment unaware of its cocoon. Though of course there's the passivity of reflection that we of the west ignore.

You'll never be at ease in love for the simple reason that you seek an ideal. Now your ideal, being unique, by definition can't be found in another. All dies and passes: plans, youth, genius, love, combats, worries, works, and simple hearts. All passes and dies: young people with gorgeous genitals in decay, day and night and life and death die. A ship can sink at daybreak. What we've waited for all our life can come and go away without our recognition. Deceptions, disappointments disappear and die as well. . . . And my ultimate reaction is of great disappointment. Then, too, I'm a little scared of you. You, you, you! *Oh, toi!!* Otototototototototoi!!!

Easter Sunday. Awful hangover. Awful cold. Awful aches and pains from yesterday's excesses on 28th Street, awful heat. Finally will be the approach of an end to something when you no longer need worry about where your next screw is coming from. "And why? Have I been too much loved," I wrote in June of '52. "I think I have been too much loved, and a little success is the same as a lot."

One reason the collapse of a romance is boring to outsiders
(not to mention participants) is that it contradicts both natural
structure and the structure of art, a postcoital paralysis that
disintegrates rather than builds, and goes on too long. The end
of love is like the *Boléro* played backward.

He's too "sure" of himself to progress, ego too solid for
amelioration. But egotism's fine and positive when it doesn't
harm others—sometimes even when it does. Now however he
tells himself: "I no longer love. I'll write a letter, and that will fix
everything." Fix everything! Obsessed with detail, he sees nothing whole. What made him think out of bed no one took him
seriously? Fix everything! The letter's sewn total disorder. We
can only see things as we see them. Your red is my green. The
redder it seems for you the redder it stays, a red decided since
your first infant red (or in any case the red you *think* you see),
and one can't change reds in midstream. My green stays, alas,
my green! Certain puzzles nevertheless suddenly solve themselves: the answer smacked us so hard we couldn't feel it. They
showed me a million other greens I'd never suspected, and
several were even stained with red. And you—do you see them?

Rejected—*plaqué*—atrocious word. Admittedly of course I
rationalize, ball you out, sing your praises while looking, looking
for an urgent alley of explication, while the plain truth is that I
miss you insanely. Tomorrow therefore, and wrongly, I'll buy a
ticket to Paris, where I'll pretend to be indifferent. You see?
. . . I'm less deceived by your attitudes about love than by your
ignorance of friendship, your blind good conscience, by the risks
you run without running risks. For instance, our last morning in
Holland you said: "Well, tonight we go back. The pain if you
said what a nice outing, and now *adieu!*" Tables turn. You speak
in formulas as you act. I'd not understood, that night in Pigalle,
when you said a *voyage à deux* would be determining, for
usually others tired of you in a fortnight; I'd not understood that
"others" meant yourself. Not understood that, like 90 percent,
you existed through habit by surrounding with halos all passing

excitements. But to have humiliated me! I've thought too much about you lately to have anything left to say when next we're face to face.

Why did you come to America if you knew from the start you hated me? A demolishing Columbus needs funds. It's curious, even amusing, how two beings tonight are intimate as twin embryos and tomorrow as distant icebergs. You were the first to say *je t'aime* and the first *à rompre*. Show your photo to another person and risk losing a bit of yourself; show a whole scrapbook and you'll lose the other person as well. Happily life starts (or starts up again) when love starts up again (or starts), and it's unimportant (*et tant mieux*) that these actions reflect themselves infinitely. I've said I love you to I don't know how many, each time was the first, and each sincere. For the "always" of lovers is a Time set apart and out of daily usage. One has time for everything if one wants: being busy's a pallid excuse. You'll see when you grow up. When I grow up I'll have lost curiosity. Anger begins to replace languor, it's health, are you glad or not? There remains simply the question of faith.

In a dream last night an infant, dark and adorable, has his tongue ripped out *without warning* by bandits. I care for him, curing, cajoling, and his trust returns. Now Gilles de Rays fondled them *before* the torture, so if one succeeded in surviving, his faith wouldn't necessarily return at the same time. It's up to you to see the relationship. . . . If you knew how I still vainly wait for your impossible note, indirect news, even a phone call. For two months and twelve days you've been gone, not even disliking me, and you're still here squelching each minute. *Je t'aime.*

In Bernard Rogers' opera, Delilah blinds Samson with white-hot pokers, then asks: And how do things look now? In *The Big Sleep* Humphrey Bogart says: They knock your teeth out, then accuse you of stammering! How's your quiet conscience? All

around I see the same drastic mistakes re-procreating themselves
as if adults never had time to learn from their children. In just
two weeks I take a plane for Orly despite awaiting perils. I'm
afraid of nothing. But rumors of war thrill me less than the
thought of seeing you. (We'll know the answer in three minutes.) You dissimulate your game so well! Not a game? Yes it is:
silence is already a game. I lied from the start. The result
sickened and cured me. We've never been friends. Just lovers a
little, never friends.

Quite sick and full of codeine. The smell of your sleep
awakened me. Hysteria's turned to disgust. Kissing is a waste of
time. My strength is stronger than myself. I've a terror of being
forgotten, from which comes the strength, stronger than me,
preventing fear of being forgotten, etc. The Nordic says love me
or I'll kill myself. The Latin says love me or I'll kill you. . . . It
was not the palpable You I loved but a shadow's shadow I
walked beside as with a cadaver on those *boulevards de l'ex-
térieur.* Sweet memories will always be soiled by your action.
Loving afternoons on the banks of the Marne before we met are
preferable now. And you name me cloying because I'd rather be
called angel than bitch. My life did not start and stop with you;
it did, however, stop and start with you. I know of torments
better than movies to distract you. End what you begin. Faithful
to a type. You were intimidating because we never laughed.
Love commences with shock and continues through habit. Six
years ago I wrote: I'm the image of love, not the thing itself, and
can't be slept with more than statues, though one takes statues to
bed with faces impassive and shoulders stony. Which is why I
weep, stones weep, because I was granted all, not part, and all
can't be shared. Only the incomplete can enjoy love.

It's you who were mistaken, I remain consistent in still
adoring you. It's up to you—the reparation gesture. . . . He
said: "I love you, I love you, I love you, excuse me, I have a

date, and anyway I've changed my mind." Watch out! Before you jump from high stone wings aim straight or your fickle blood will infect the pool of neighboring swimmers and you too. . . . You were the flop of my life, meaning: my own flop—as though you said: I was the flop in Ned's life. Ironically I no longer remember the names or faces of so many whose hearts withered through me. There's our justice!

Still ill as a dog, sinus infection, high fever, wandering about watching the quick flame of spring fertilize Manhattan, which bursts each moment into hot emeralds, all suddenly more close and precious, as always, now that I'm so soon leaving. The great heats, jonquil orgies on Park Avenue, and Central Park's again a cathedral of green lace over croaking kids and whining frogs in crocuses which strike at the heart like rattlesnakes, and the sky has a cloudless yellow smile as I've grown fond of someone who aches at my leaving and will maybe be glad when I return next fall.

Instantly there I am fortuitously precipitated into a monster gulf, a void, scabs ripped from the wound. Gradually the gulf fills up, with our own blood, blood of dizzy forgetfulness, a bit melancholy. Such are the ways of nature. A public cherub. With that face of yours *on te donnerait le bon Dieu sans confession.* But let's recall Marie Laure's first word at your photo. *Sadique!* . . . I remark, seeing someone in the street, *je serais bien dans ses bras.* You remark, *ça serait bien dans mes bras.* So who's a mirror? And you're quickly discouraged. I've never been in so many beds as during these last ten weeks. You never especially pleased me physically, love seldom can. I'm quite another person from the one you last saw. A week from this afternoon the plane leaves for France. Lou Harrison has always seemed to me America's most *inspired* composer. Paris will disintoxicate these blue thoughts. We're all just customers to you.

Tomorrow I go to Paris. With a camera's accuracy I recall mirthlessly every minute we spent together. Am feeling little friendship for you now, letting myself be so guided by the heart, but was it really to the detriment of work?

Paris, chez Marie Laure

Well!! We've met again. Last evening. *Nous avons même fait l'amour.* And though it didn't work too brilliantly (as you say) it was not so much from my shyness as your casualness. Yet I think we both were moved, that you were even lonely and would start up again (on quite another foot, of course—we're no longer the same people, etc.). Maybe I'm wrong. You know, I rather despised you later? All the same, in the taxi home there was sorrow caused by the strange-familiar streets of your far part of town, your slaughterhouses of La Villette, the heavenly prison of blue Paris again. I'd sworn never to confront you with injustices, nor will I (*d'ailleurs* you'd shield yourself French-style) since vengeance is not a strong point. But neither will I ever tell you my true feelings. But will tell you this because you want to know: yes, I still love you (what a dull word now) but with a love denuded of gentleness, one doesn't feel gentle toward the heel of a shoe. So much was, and will remain, unsaid. No doubt best. I only ask to see you amicably, painlessly from time to time. But yes, I detest you somewhat. So take it easy for God's sake, you are a careful surgeon after all, and your hand's too magic on the flesh—don't step in those screwy corners of my lungs.

I'm not sorry you didn't suffer, Claude; I'm only surprised you think you're incapable of suffering. But you don't give yourself time. Try. Less masochist than a sleepwalker. (Though I've seen you suffer.) Anyway *I* have, and can't begin again as though nothing had happened. Do my ears deceive me! You speak of trips to Rome, joint excursions to the *fête à la* Place de la Nation or the Château de Vincennes! Remember my memory and wait a while. . . . Yes, I was tempted to write you. But you never answered my last (the one that began with the passion of Hungary), and besides, what's the use? On the other hand I wrote all these slobbery pages with the half-veiled notion that

one day you'd look. And you will, maybe not right away, maybe
with a little embarrassment and a lot of boredom because you
won't find yourself but you'll find me and understand the
privilege of contradictions uttered in self-defense to keep me
breathing. . . . Do you know what touched me most last night?
When you said: "No one phones unless they've got a toothache."
Know that I'm here, like you, am glad to see you, have some
things that belong to you.

I've no more time to lose with those who don't pay me court.
It was myself who made me suffer, not you; myself who was able
to endure the purge, not you. Anyone else could have been an
indirect cause. Not you.

June 1st. Eight years ago today I first came to France. I miss
your conversation and your arms. Close up the worst and give of
yourself, everyone. It's only innocent people who feel the need to
justify themselves.

Oh, this wonderful hot weather! Beauties come out now on
the streets, *débraillées,* and Paris light stays until nearly ten in
the evening (and dawn is at three) with a lemonade glow, and
the streets seething with the nervous and happy. The season
changes, bringing the past like a flashlight into the Chicago
parks where, as an adolescent, I lay (ignorant of danger: hence
safe) in the arms of adults smelling of sun and gasoline and
strength, the spring human smell of the *débraillé.* . . . When
was it? Where have they gone? Today we have lunch in the
garden. I go to the movies, one cannot be an amateur of both
theater and cinema: I choose the movies.

For nineteen years I have been making love. Eva Gauthier
used to tell her male singing students: "Just be glad you're not a
soprano obliged to give a recital in spite of her 'period' when
with every high note she feels blood rushing downward and
prays that the audience is unaware of the red puddle forming on
the floor." . . . These steaming spring evenings what else can

we think of? love and sex along the river bridges. I'm different in summer than in winter, different in Paris than New York. And I see the arms around that little boy grow tighter, smaller, more distant, and somehow I'm no longer jealous of my childhood.

The heart—his heart—will shrink in its safety vault; I can't begrudge that unconsciousness, any more than the little bitch of *The Bad Seed*, the final revenge for my indifferent innocence. The *petit bourgeois* of the 19th Arrondissement, hobnobbing with artists and playing Don Juan, can now go stew in his own juice. Because we see each other as monsters, each unfair to the other. Kick me in the mouth like Bogart. I've too much heart, and you: none. (But am your equal in bad manners.) One doesn't torture another almost to death only to be later merely vexed that the "victim" misunderstood. You pushed to the utmost limits, cat and mouse, exasperated. From self-protection here's the definitive break. I've had you again and am not interested. Therefore I dump you—*je te plaque*. As conquest I cost you plenty. It's always a mistake to show one's love too much. You bastard.

These are the calmest, the least mean words with which to end this letter addressed to a misunderstanding. How changed a person I've become only someone else will tell. But I would rather have as remembrance the smell of those arms in a Chicago park tighten sharp around me nineteen years ago again tonight in the heat of France. *Salaud! Espèce de maquereau!* You pig, You real pig! You bad damn son-of-a-bitch, you prick. You shit!

PART 6

Paris, Italy, Hyères, Paris, New York

Summer–Autumn 1957

La maladie de l'Europe est de ne croire à rien et de prétendre tout savoir.

—CAMUS, *Réflexions sur la Guillotine*

Paris, July

Again tonight in the heat of France. Intelligent waste. Some wise mistakes:

When I reread this it will be cold somewhere, months, years, from here. But this evening I seem alive by myself and can't believe the risks I've run. More like a nun alone at sundown through the cloister garden for the ten-thousandth time thinking on her first arrival: same trees, same grass, same sun, new nun (old nun). That's how it goes, as we grow on, not learning much, stopping dead in our tracks: the honest man this morning may murder tonight, just as now the lush on self-patrol may yet be drunk again so soon; the atrocious example of others is useless, *on se fait des raisons*. I carefully build my health up to a weekly breakdown. Year in and out this pattern's gone on too long, and what once had elements of fun is now sterile humiliation, demolishing, *ennui* (but drinking too starts from nervous habit of boredom). It's as though I self-imposed an impediment to hamper work, slow down life. And the reconstructive week of movie-going (oh! nothing with *shooting!* think of our headache!), I've said it all before, still start and start again. Kell Kweet! If I am an alcoholic I still hate to drink. Even more, I hate myself when I drink.

Again tonight in the heat of Paris, hot Tuileries fountains surrounded by wire chairs upside-down in lights from the ice-cream shacks, heated flowers in darkness, and wandering

couples, the mad long streak of summer lanterns all the way up
to l'Etoile. I spoke with a stranger there, but it led to nothing.

▼▼▼

Concert of my music at the American Embassy. Because
soprano Ethel Semser's nice leg was in a plaster cast she could
not walk. We therefore kept the curtain down, posed Ethel
beside the piano like a statue in an evening gown, and were both
on stage when the curtain rose. Then, my God, it wasn't us but
the audience which seemed on display as we gazed out over that
Proustian assemblage of heads.

▼▼▼

Composing, since I have become a "professional," has long
since ceased to be a spontaneous gesture, but a laborious responsibility needing more reflection than the youthful inspiration we
take for granted.

I like the image of Saturday night in a packed city bar outside
of which there is only prairie for a thousand miles. And I like
those who stay home rehearsing for days so that they may come
and "sight-read" before respectful auditors of the intimate chamber music gathering. . . . All told, and in the long run, it's the
old proved classics which move us the most when we still take
time to listen instead of hearing with more careful ears the glitter
of our own modern music almost snowed under by the sciences.
But, too, the classics are what truly bore us the most.

▼▼▼

I rather detest with good reason (the stronger that they are
beloved) these seven: Hemingway, Eartha Kitt, Schweitzer,
Samuel Beckett, Joan of Arc, Casals, and June Allyson.

▼▼▼

Just had the first polio shot because if I hadn't and got
infantile paralysis I'd kick myself. Or as Joe LeSueur pointed

out: "If you *could* kick yourself!" Joe, who has written a book called *Answering a Question in the Mountains*.

▼▼▼

For three weeks I've been back, though not back. Yet no longer either in America, but at some midpoint without a particular happiness or sadness, a little bored, no strong *goût de vivre* nor anything settled to look sentimentally forward to. Still Paris is flaming with those wild spring storms that smell of summer while I take long unfocused walks alone to dispel the fourth hangover. At least now I've resolved as well as it can be done the problem for which I've arrived—that louse—and would be ready tomorrow to go back to New York, if it wasn't a waste of money, toward a grass no greener on the other side of the ocean. I'd also be ready to fall blindfolded into a brand-new affair, credulous, passive, jealous and demanding: *l'amour, quoi!* Meanwhile I write song after song on poems of Elizabeth Bishop, and see that although France has somehow gone on without me, it's also reawakening like the sleeping princess at my return. France doesn't know she gives no more escapes to someone, older, for whom pedestrians no longer turn around much. That's why we write diaries: to scold a public which doesn't react.

Feeling lonely. No one writes, nor telephones. It's dark and raining, depressed without tension, a need for anticipation. Few ideas, a little reading (Bernard Minoret, E. M. Forster). A head full of tuneless songs. The truth is I haven't yet come back to life. *Nullement sauvage, j'ai horreur d'être seul. Je me sens malade.*

▼▼▼

Write a poem on the ruses of cruising, fears in the street, long strolls seeking those who run away, "looking for love where it can't be found and waiting for love where it will not come," how to evade with the happy foreknowledge of being caught, how to reject gracefully and ungraciously, etc. And call it: The Art of the Fugue.

▼▼▼

Americans build toward the sky, the French make love toward the earth. The French (visual but unmusical) create a snobism about the harpsichord, which is dry and precise, but around the harp (blurred and luscious) no snobism can be built, for sensuality—though we fear it today—is popular. There is a repellent female approach saying: "Music is a privilege, a relaxation." It is not a privilege but on anyone's doorstep; not a relaxation but a positive ear-opener for the auditor willing to work at letting go and forgetting the less complex structure of mouth and eye. This I have explained in Philadelphia to Edna Phillips. To my father, weary of the rivalry and altercations of communal work and desirous of joining an "outfit" that knows its own mind and functions as one, I explain: "How can an *outfit* know what it wants? By definition it is made of mind-groups no two of which can ever truly agree." Our earth is the same, but I believe it's the only one we've got.

I am still convalescing. That is why this pale enthusiasm is just nourished by watery broth and no spermy ink. Art (that!) is simply a series of inevitably correct but accidental choices. [Explain why *He has come over a toy sky to find me* is a distortion from myopia that formed grace.]

▼▼▼

Marc Blitzstein in New York took the time to help me translate my libretto to *The Robbers* from (as he said) English into English. Since then I like the work less but Marc more. Menotti has let me see that one of my songs is worth the whole opera.

Let's translate *l'amour est terrible* by Love is Terrible. The distortion is amusing, and thus two nationalities are angrily fused.

Le Partage de midi is a combination of *Camino Real* and Rita

Hayworth's old movie *Gilda.* Its greatness keeps it from vulgarity, its sensuality from tedium. And of course *la Feuillère* is
today's best actress as actresses (*les belles fausses*) go. Who
wants real life? Good theater in its form and concentration
improves on God. If you know a lot of people it's easier to
replace them.

▼▼▼

I've been back in France four weeks. Still not back, etc. But
l'épisode Claude is over and closed with the ugliest finish
imaginable. I have no more force to note the details (though
when I spit in his face a molar fell out!), nor does it make any
difference. Yet I think often of it with a heavy heart, and still
feel lonely. I'm lonely because I know too many people, and
pacify myself by writing letters, it's my habit: the literature of
separation. Drinking too much. No sex (nor feel the need,
though feel I should feel it). I grow confounded by the intimacy
of such acts where two bodies strive so tragically to be one, and
the empty-stranger post-orgasm abyss. It happened last night:
the frenzied pathetic joy of a child before his birthday cake,
followed by the tears of abandonment when the last guest is
gone. I'm ready for the calm assurance of a single person, the
thatched hut, a cabbage patch.

▼▼▼

It's chilly for June and river lights have no heat in the wind.
We can only see ourselves when away from home. Gide's
funeral was nearly seven years ago and all Paris seemed in
mourning. Could it happen that way in America for *any* man of
letters (even Hemingway)? Prokosch told me yesterday he
needs to live far from America's "vulgarity." Now I no longer
(nor did I ever) see it this way, and want more and more to
leave the France I know as well as my pocket through which I've
suffered. And I'm bored, and bored, bored.

J'ai le cafard.
J'ai le cafard (another day).
J'ai un peu moins le cafard.
J'ai le cafard.
At least our friends console us by growing simultaneously older and recalling like yesterday those popular songs of the thirties.

▼▼▼

It's early in the morning. *J'ai découché.* It's my Robert Hillyer song. It's hot, *et je ne le fais jamais.* I relive my songs, though I'm not always sure of the poem's meaning as I write the music. I compose not through past experience but what *will* happen to me. Today I create (not *the,* but) my future—and, years after, I whistle my own tunes while practicing what they preach.

▼▼▼

Some people recover, improve, and advance: Nell Tangeman, after a session in Saint Vincent's, is now a new and glowing person. Some people relapse, disintegrate, and sink: Boris, after dubious years of secret Russian charm and a *litre* of pernod per day, is now a bloated mass of scabs in his tuxedo mumbling like a forgotten moron. Some people seem to stay the same through the years, and they are frequent, frequent. Those who advance, learn and work with flying saucers. Boris lives on the Rue Bleue, between the Rue de Paradis and the Rue Papillon; lovely names, but the *arrondissement* is overrun with Arab assassins. It is very hot and rainy, a late Sunday afternoon. My eyes look out on a level with the treetops and my head and heart swim with an overuse of alcohol these last fainting days. Overpreoccupation with detail, trimming to perfection, is only laziness. But the performance of a Schubert trio must be a *ménage à trois sans bagarre* which, in real life, just doesn't exist. My breakfast is of red foods: apples and peppers, cherries and tomatoes, strawberries and rare meat. In which category do I fall?

▼▼▼

Since leaving school nearly ten years ago I have lived more or less exactly as I pleased (have I been pleased?): going to bed and getting up when I feel like it; answering to no higher boss (similar to my friends in art—though not to those in romance who've been obliged to keep my schedule, thereby falling ill); living where I wish, seeing and eating who and what I want; writing the music I hear; desiring to have what I desire when I desire (from the very start I was a spoiled child); enough money, no real material fears; overdrinking, but with the time always to "sleep it off." Now, with this mass of leisure I have, through the years with a Protestant order, accomplished more in sheer mileage (if not in quality) than any other leisured innocent I know—living immoderately on both sides of the scale, but with an almost desperate sentimental restraint. And I have been reasonably happy. And I have been reasonably "successful" (by American standards). The beautiful have a more drastic challenge than the ugly in aging, for only they must habituate to a change.

▼▼▼

Day after tomorrow, the Mistral for Toulon, leaving thus the anonymous peace of a big city for my routine summer industry. The heat wave of this past week has been the strongest in France for eighty years: all one can do is lie around, reading a great deal in a suffocated semisleep which is rather pleasant. Nobody and nothing interests me, though at least in my present state of convalescence I can again concentrate on a page or an air-cooled movie screen. The heat. Already six, seven, eight years back I was lunching with Caïds in the Moroccan desert, blond as the sun, while the weeks slipped by invisibly. Am I only capable of a passion in lost causes?

What comfort is there in pederasty to one who's not a creator? In love, something more than just itself must be an issue. Since the war we've come away from three thousand years of art into an age of science where flying saucers as easily nourish intelligent souls. Young American composers today are early-married professors with steady incomes and no further need of competition, writing square works for their babies. Only I (ten years older than they), poor, but living in a French house of luxury, seem out of joint suddenly in what I sing. But if I am "not of this time," couldn't it be *au contraire* that I feel this Today so well and much I've got to leave?

My last largest works I've escaped and never heard: the Second Symphony, the Woodwind Sinfonia, *The Robbers* will sing first without me in September California. Does my logical intelligence eliminate a sense of taste? "Good taste" has never (like courage and sincerity) been of my concerns. Taste, like intelligence, can lessen the necessary abandon of creation, though intelligence and taste have nothing to do with each other. I've no taste. But intelligence wants me to keep this diary when I should be musicalizing. And I read too much. Ought to fornicate more (now while it's still available to my age)—I feel the need—instead of talking about it, walking the streets and combing my hair for it, left unsatisfied like a strangled belch.

▼▼▼

Hyères

What a reassuring pleasure it is, summer after summer while the world goes to pot and sizzles there in precipitous change, to hear in the marketplace and alleys the Provençal language still being spoken and even by seven-year-olds who weren't born when I first saw this town.

Faisons le bilan! During just three weeks in Hyères I have completed two symphonic movements and God knows how many songs, including a short cycle on Whitman poems for Wilder Burnap and his virginals! "I pour the stuff to start sons . . ." wrote Walt; and now, with a brand-new friend (PQ, medical botanist and physical *mélange* of Jean Lagrolet, Dane Clark, and Noel Lee, with a *visage crépusculaire* which climbs me like a tree but leaves me limp), I'm off on a car trip to the isles of Naples.

We leave Saturday. . . . We are what we make of ourselves; artists are "makers of manners"; could I be that composer who remains, for love, always in France? In any case today it's the only country of conversations, and here in Hyères at Marie Laure's we are living amongst the pleasantest company of our century.

French society consists of those who pronounce (Lord and Minoret), those who are pronounced upon (*les dames du monde*), and those who sum it up with *le don de la réplique* (Cocteau, Noailles, or the middle-class talents: Mauriac, Bourdet, etc.). For years Marie Laure called me Miss Sly, the foreign absorber. To myself I seem the sole remaining Romantic, a languisher, moving through black mornings or anguished dusks with an ardent wish for awakening into another dimension. It's not a female impersonator's name—like Miss Citronella Snowdrift—but rather a title for one of Father Divine's humorless daughters.

The Italian trip will help to take up and sort souvenirs as a box of colored candy, as the sumptuous order which only lady authors—Colette and Woolf—feel. With a certain relief I see disappearing the *joli garçon* I used to be (I used to take my own breath away), while dipping (how gracefully!) into the thirties' duties. Beauties have two lives: the old, the young. Uglies stay always the same, no matter how smart, and will not hear that embarrassing knock on the door of orgasm—or just when you sit down with a book on the toilet the phone rings (it's never anyone nice either). I knew I was grown up before anybody suspected; I remain a child with no one knowing. I understood grown-ups as a child (I have nothing of my own Corinthians), and today can see a child as clearly as day before yesterday. How different these lives and aims, among all my lovers, a spider-web railroad leading and lost into the desert.

I am never idle. *Les vacances c'est là où on travaille ailleurs,* said Colette, and sunlight with sand for me must be accompanied by letters of order and hot thought.

Il faut cultiver sa légende.

▼▼▼

Auric recounts the cremation of his Protestant colleague, my former master, Honegger, the first of *les Six* to die. A coffin, like any other, is lowered into an oven in full view of the collected mourners. The door is closed as upon a final act at the Folies Bergères full of flowers, and a dull burning machine sounds in the distance. Eulogies begin, speeches, epitaphs with tears. Twenty minutes. The minister motions to a choirboy who opens the door, looks down the shaft, shakes his head, withdraws. Not ready yet! Nervous silence. Another speech . . . Finally the coffin, shrunk to the size of an urn, is given to Madame Honegger, who holds in this jewel box the body of her husband.

▼▼▼

Telegram from Charles-Henri Ford. Tchelichew is dead. Gone in an Italian summer like Latouche a year ago, the end of one friendship as long and desultory as the other. What can we remark anymore about these recurrences which increasingly attack our own selves? A bit of me too is gone with Pavlik.

It was as long ago as 1945 that I implored Parker Tyler to introduce us. The fantasies at the Modern Museum were haunting me as was the painter's own head glimpsed across a room and mythological. Parker arranged a *dîner à trois* at the Russian Tea Room, but I was shy and Pavlik ailing (older than I'd expected); I recall nothing but his river of talk, the red ribbon on his wrist "to ward off evil spirits," and his surprise that Parker had brought him "a child." A year later I wrote music for a puppet show called "At Noon Upon Two" authored by Charles-Henri, designed by Kurt Seligmann, manipulated by John Myers, presented at the Old Knickerbocker on Second Avenue, and attended by everyone of those days including Pavlik, who said on seeing me, "My God, he's an old man now." I was twenty-one.

Our final meeting was last year in Frascati when P. and I went for lunch and saw nothing but Charles-Henri's pictures. And now what is there? I feel sick, for no special reason.

▼▼▼

Hubert de Saint Senoch and Charles Hathaway come around occasionally. They own a pair of Rolls-Royces. The larger is for visiting duchesses. The smaller (to avoid ostentation) is for cruising the *bas fonds* of Toulon.

▼▼▼

September. Who seeing Paestum for the first time would not wish to die there? It rips out the blood and the Greeks have peacefully won, they remain, while the Roman ruins aren't crumbled but melted like ice cream. . . . It's a month later (retrospective journals are less fun but easier) and, Yes, I spent August in Italy with PQ. If nothing else, it purged and scraped me clean of that gray anguish in the Spring of Claude.

The mountain comes to Mohammed.

This was my eleventh trip into Italy and in three weeks we did 4,000 kms. in PQ's Dauphine. Dark, a cloudy lover settles like a storm on top of me. Can I only only like *that*? (Yet certainly I'm growing no younger.) All my gorgeous honeymoons, and that regular magical hour of the meal with a lover. I am dying not to die. I repeat: what we learned from our last love affair teaches us what *not* to do in the next; yet when the next is over we realize that what we refrained from doing was, in this case, just the thing we *should* have done. Now can this help itself from being again the summer romance which fades like a suntan in the fall? A professor of botany has concrete duties and only artists can afford folly. But *justement* they are alone in their folly.

▼▼▼

Amalfi

Silver stalactites. And all this world's history oozing from the old Mediterranean's importance; what was I, an Anglo-Saxon, doing there? Being in love? There's nothing to cure that. Near Genoa we look at the sunset as powdered rust sprinkled onto blue whip-cream. Rome: thick ivory sun on the orange city where the always unbelievable Italians wash their cars in the spray of Saint Peter's fountains. And PQ is shocked if, with a whore's address, I enter the treasury room at Saint Peter's and say: *Ciào tesoro!* But pays no true attention to me: we get along fine, but I could as well be anyone else and not Ned Rorem: I could even be the Miss Millay of my childhood saying (what was it?) "I am in love with him to whom the Hyacinth is dearer than I shall ever be dear." But it's my first botanist, for whom I'll one day be as dusty as Pompei. Gardens. Hans Werner Henze showing us the sights of Naples says in his special French: *"Et voilà le jardin méchant!"*—which of course has nothing to do with botany, but which can neither break our hearts like a sunset on the Appian Way (what poem as a child did I write of "Five O'Clock on a Roman Road"?) nor bleach the souvenir of my palm on the driver's thigh.

Capri's a work of the devil, Paestum and Ravello seem nearly things of God, but Rome shows that as usual the best work's done by man. Go into Florence's Accademia and know why Valéry was right to say "A work of art is never completed: it is abandoned." Not abandoned are the life-sized statues in Florence's cemetery: tasteful Carrara marble replicas of the deceased in Ginger-Rogers-type 1930's pageboy bobs. Where do I go from here? And in love? What love affair has ever not been impossible? The hills of Rome as breasts are brave little pears, but often Nature makes a mistake when she thought up love affairs. We are more forsaken than the ship *Mary Celeste* in 1872.

The actual truth is that, except for an occasional song, writing music rather bores me. It is a necessary chore, and the wisest are the laziest. Control of laziness is a secret to success, but composition of tears is given only to a few despite themselves. Knowing, then, that I must "make," what *is* it I seem to crave as well? A need to share? Nevertheless, the constant molding of attainment toward romance as I seem to want it keeps me in a state of tension preventing work. And still I work. That's how it is.

The Big Dipper couldn't care less. "Controlling" our nature, we do the same to music: do you suppose a phrase is happy knowing it falls into a 12-tone orbit? Or that a tone is less lonely to find that it has overtones? You can't go home again (but you can, I have). No traveler returns. And no one really has more than himself.

▼▼▼

Monologue of a Fairly Young Composer. Gardens Without Pity (Nîmes). Deception deeper than heaven, and hellish as the Aven d'Orgnac. Why do I write all that? Because yesterday evening I returned again to Hyères from a five-day excursion, with PQ, of Provence and Languedoc. Where weren't we? The same almost as Henry James' little tour of France. In any case it's not possible to go farther from a skyscraper than to the *manade* of Jean Lafont. Imagine (*au Cailar* where his Toril and tiny half-finished house are) dining by lamplight in the dark chilly garden. Five yards off, the end of the universe. At midnight a full moon, and we go to watch the sleep of two hundred kneeling bulls in a fog thicker than butter and *Boris Godounov* sings from the radio. That's where Jean Lafont lives with an adopted adolescent. *Je n'invente rien.* And discretion's a quality more precious than the sugar of sincerity or noblesse; with it, any life can be led.

Masterpieces are all boring. It takes time to appreciate the syntax of new loves. But at least in Arles or Avignon or Aix I've made love. In *Mes Apprentissages* there's a letter from Jean Lorrain, who says, *"Oui, le hâle fait les yeux bleus plus bleus,*

mais l'amour en Provence les cerne comme nulle part ailleurs!"
Leave Arles, leave the cloisters of St. Trophime, les Alyscamps,
the theater and dangerous arena, leave Arles for the remains of
Mont Majour nearby, where you'll smell honey so thick that the
sound of bees, the sound of yellow, is in the fragrance. Do it
with a lover. Look at Daudet's windmill if you wish (from a
distance) and lunch at Saint Rémy after a visit to the high
mausoleum which the peasants of that region call *Les Antiques*;
this too is far from skyscrapers. Buy some candy at the springs of
Vaucluse, and as you chew try thinking of Laura and Petrarch if
you're not too nervous for your lover. Les Baux is worth an
afternoon, and the Val de l'Enfer. Then go to sleep in Avignon
or Villeneuve d'Avignon, but do it with a lover. The beds are
good. Next morning in Orange there's the orange Roman theater
(and a triumphal arch), but later at Vallon is the incomparable
nature's Pont d'Arc (Utah has no equal) where you can take a
river swim in the Ardèche (naked), then the grottos of Orgnac,
and along the roadside *les Dolmens,* where the Gauls sacrificed
their friends a thousand years before Christ said not to. Uzès,
where Racine lived a while. And oh, the Pont du Gard. In the
evening at the Nîmes arena watch a game of Rugby with a live
bull added for complication, laugh with a lover. And go to bed
and quarrel. Montpellier with the esplanade Peyrou, and far out
of town hidden near the wild beaches is the old church of
Maguélone. Have lunch in the ugly resort of Palavas on PQ's
birthday (Sept. 9), then take a train back alone to Toulon with
tears in your eyes.

▼▼▼

I cannot wait until tonight to say I love you.
Now Marie Laure has forbidden me to write letters. She's
right. Their wings catch fire and spray friends with ashes.
Yet I must, and will do it here. New friend, you'll admire my
silence when we meet again to say good-bye in Paris. *Donc:*

[Here follows, believe it or not, a forty-page treatise addressed to PQ between the time of our Provençal excursion and our farewell season in Paris a few weeks later. I have neither the patience nor the esthetic to translate and reproduce it here. Suffice it to say that Marie Laure, after reading both this and the letter to Claude, commented simply: "I'd put both those people in a box, tie it with a ribbon, and throw it in the deep blue sea."—N.R. 1967]

▼▼▼

Knowing I go Thursday to Paris, and now is Monday, I've already left, yet still here time drags by at a snail's pace. More trying than an arrival too soon. Meanwhile I've not had a drink for two months and roast myself all naked daily in the last sun, for the Île-de-France will be cold they say. I compose and onanize and read, liking my Third Symphony, the human body firm and fragile as a paperclip.

Boris Kochno mailed from Switzerland a letter in lovely script to Marie Laure in which he speaks of himself in the third person as someone met on a beach who asked after her—but he was unable to reply. My friend Jean Leuvrais solves such puzzles irrefutably: those he admires or loves he makes a part of his life whether they know it or him or not; he works the strings of people a hemisphere away—their least decision has his approval. He's not bothered with the flesh. News flash: Nature improves on art.

▼▼▼

Paris, early autumn 1957

Yes, I've come back to Paris two nights ago and have already had my homecoming *cuite* of disgrace, face a bit hacked, which comes (as we know) from the jerky shaving with a hangover. Cities, cities, cities as doll-town mazes. My hand's still none too solid and the Paris air is heavy, cool, dark. I am blond, depressed, tan. If, like they say, I have no living "sense of theater" it shows more in the dying sense of compulsive occasional drinking. Everyone has his particular *sens de théâtre,* which is not necessarily the sense of *spectacle. Au fond* I'm really a very good person and too credulous. Sick of suffering: there's been too much; and I long for the opportunistic thrust which could help me select mates to help a career. Why not? Oh it's dark and I must go out. . . . PQ has arrived (must watch my P's and Q's!) and tonight, with J. P. Marty, we will dine. It's nervous-making. Raining hard. And Sibelius finally died today. Also the king of Norway.

▼▼▼

Yes, I've had beautiful women also in love. Now the incomparable Madame T. Perhaps after all marriage is the happy solution.

Tu es orgueilleux, mais non pas vaniteux. Chez moi c'est l'inverse. Voici la différence.

Maybe: A Symphony of Poems
Orchestrate: *Visits to Saint Elizabeth's*
Title for a painting of Dominguez: *Cercueil de Vitesse.* Noisy Coffins.

▼▼▼

In last month's *Poetry* David Posner has dedicated to me his "Poem for Music." But Paul Goodman quotes my style in last year's learned review *I. E.*

▼▼▼

Looking back—now that three seasons have come and gone—at that endless letter to Claude (and it was only one of the many not sent), I feel both embarrassment and impatience. I now see myself as a self-indulgent nag, in view of what I've since learned (do we learn?). True, that suffering was close to unendurable, though in viewing it now (but one doesn't "view it now"—such things freeze) my anxiety was less from love or even privation than from insult, an insult spewing a blank year of recovering from two months of bliss. Still, is time lost in mourning time lost?

Today I marvel only at the energy of that sorrow. No mention, however, is made of my Third Symphony, begun and completed that summer. It's bemusing to consider the lacunae in musical subject matter here. In that whole winter's writing to Claude not only did I seldom allude to other persons, but in a hallucination of one-track-mindedness there was complete omission of the news that *The Poets' Requiem* (then my most extended work) had its world premiere.

▼▼▼

Like God, made in our image, we endow those we love with imagined timeless qualities which they neither possess nor (usually) want us to think they possess. When, then, our disillusion of necessity arrives as we witness the collapse we've forced upon them (but for which we take no responsibility), we hate them; and, like God, they can only stare back with that blank surprised dismay of corpses.

▼▼▼

While sipping anisette on the terrace of the Royal Saint Germain we see Jean Genet stroll by on the arm of DeNoël, to whom he is saying: *"Mon Dieu,* since that damn book came out [Sartre's *Saint Genêt*] I can't even pick my nose in public without someone whispering 'Oh, that gesture refers to so and so and you can read about it on page such and such,' and so I . . ." and his voice trails off as they disappear into the crowd, for he never sits down. But we sip more anisette, and observe the next passersby.

▼▼▼

In thirty-six hours I leave in a plane for America. Here it feels as though winter's come. The weather's made our Paris world like a cave. Will I come back with the buds? As all grows smaller we still spread out. PQ goes to Algiers. Now we pass our days doing Seine things: the old Venus de Milo and the Gioconda smile (ripe ladies when I was a child) appear adolescent today. Works of art do change; not because we become more intelligent but because we grow older. Writers have always influenced me more than musicians. And who's done more than I in music for American poetry? Why doesn't Carnet do a movie of me? and write a score for my own soliloquies, precise with contrasts and all bars down—like the Balinese.

Yes, going away once more. Good-bye and good-bye, can it ever stop? Will I have another American cold season writing letters to North Africa? No: suffering *can* be controlled: when it starts, think of your toenails. Work's no real answer, but replacement or substitution are.

I've written as much as I can.

▼▼▼

New York

Thursday October the third the sun came up over Europe as usual, only I wasn't there any longer to see it. Being now in America with no New York lodgings, and the Philharmonic's opening concert canceled for the first time since Lincoln's assassination (*Design* will not be played), I wonder to what I've returned. Nevertheless, PQ, I'm glad we left Paris at the same time, each to a city the other ignores.

▼▼▼

Day after tomorrow I'll be thirty-four. Since Christ died last Easter, and I didn't, perhaps, I have a long way to go. Going professionally (or "career-wise," as they say in America) things seem fairly smooth at the moment, particularly as I am to do the music for Tennessee Williams' new one-act "shocker" *Suddenly Last Summer,* and Mitropoulos has scheduled my Woodwind Sinfonia for November 10. Also I have a place to live: back again on Thirteenth Street after thirteen years. But the ways of the heart seem null and void in this country, and though drinking bores me I do it all the same. The tenacity here, and fear and money and ambition and blindness begin by fright and finish in contagion. When have I not wished to be the direct cause of every spasm, all orgasm in the world? But so do all others now. This competition troubles because work wants quiet.

I must buy a checkerboard. And a red vase for yellow roses, a yellow vase for red roses, a red and yellow vase for roses red and yellow (as well as red vase for red roses, yellow vase for yellow roses, etc.). Would it be a good idea if Marc Blitzstein wrote a libretto for me? Last week in Bloomingdale's basement I find Grace Cohen Jaffe, beautiful Grace from the happy summer of 1946 in Tanglewood, where she says I said: "Ah, Gertrude Stein is dead. What a pity she never knew me!" Did I? Yet today don't I reproach PQ for a similar reflection in Montpellier?

▼▼▼

Dior died. I'm thirty-four.

America. I seem to be back. But how can the shock of it not shock me? Art here is more of a comedy than ever (I meant to write commodity), and anyway the twenty-year-olds—those who count—don't care, being more interested in science now; and science (except for love) has all and more than art had: mysticism and mystery and romance without sex. But I am from before and America's grown unreal. I am more and more afraid of people, and in this city of money, of comfort without luxury and violence without erection, I am lost and wondering, having never in any way prostituted myself nor dealt with people I didn't choose. How long will I last it? Until I too become hypnotized by The Big Money? But lazy habits and creative needs have now gone on too long, and we cannot even smile without paying cash for the halo-frame about the lips.

Tonight we are going (Morris and Marc Blitzstein) up to Juilliard to hear the new Copland piano piece. Why does he apologize? It's all we ever do. And the bars! Such frozenness! What couldn't I say?! At least I have . . . what was it?

▼▼▼

John Latouche: "No, I'll meet you later—after your earlier appointment. Like that you can have your date and eat it!" He used to get drunk at his own parties.

Here in American hotels are no *bidets* nor room service for breakfast. Again the Protestant shock. Take a whole bath then, every day, so as to smell better standing frozen drunk in the frozen bar and saying fearfully: no, not *this* one yet, for the next may be better. (Americans of course take too many baths.)

PART 7

New York
Spring–Summer 1958

Whoredom and wine and new wine take away the heart.

—HOSEA

Who hath woe? who hath sorrow? who hath contentions? who hath babbling? who hath wounds without cause? who hath redness of the eyes? They that tarry long at the wine.

—PROVERBS

Theme without variations. Eight months ago on my return to America I stopped writing here. And now, with winter gone and heat slapping the sexy sidewalks, I start again having nothing else to do, having finished the Third Symphony and all the rest, having stopped and recommenced and stopped with love once more, and having no plans at all. I seemed to have reached a stalemate and necessary point of reflection in work (how can I rejuvenate it?) and living (I shall not return to Europe), neither happy nor sad; though some days just the sight of a lamp, a dog, a barrel is enough to start the tears. Since normally I'm in Paris during the spring weather-change I'm moved to think of May rains the year before, but now it's been ten years, or forty seasons, since I knew New York in this season, and I think back, always back, on nearly twenty years (eighty seasons) past when in Chicago I behaved pretty much as now.

Now I know how the past gets dragged like a leaden tail. It's all red like the rain or rubies and roses and cherries and blood, sunsets and wine-drops and raspberries and Scarlet Tanagers, Cardinals and stained glass and Jello and devils, flame and hell and crimson cushions and strawberries, anger, and red as a heart. The only one I miss in Europe is myself; now that self is irretrievable, so why go back? There is nobody I particularly look forward to seeing again. The church and heaven of adults are children's former fairyland where I cannot go without serious suspicion. It's been a good ten months since I've had "satisfactory" sexual relations! Can a fish on the hook enjoy it as much as I? (But only in love.)

Dream (on the Ides of March): burning lions and horses falling in sparks from a skyscraper as I, fixed in space, look down and watch in terror those animals which were pursuing me. (It occurs that the foregoing—written in March—has the "doublings" of orchestration: the winds of "burning" is doubled by the percussion of "sparks"; the strings of "lions" by the brass of "horses"; "look down" by "watch"; "falling" by "pursuing"; etc. Doubling is dangerous: for what thickens by simultaneousness in instrumentation only confuses by redundance in prose.)

▼ ▼ ▼

Oscar Dominguez is dead. At the end of the year, to our sad astonishment, he finally fell into his own trap of threats and, across the ocean, severed wrists and ankles. The things which cannot, but *do*, happen will astound me until my own dying. Both Hart Crane and René Crevel wrote of their *type* of suicide before it happened. And so it was with our Oscar, whose souvenir I brood upon only through one tiny painting and a hundred soothing and cruel words. Why is what is prophesied never believed? Can I lump them all together like the current mode, "the sick joke," those darlings whom last winter stole while I wasn't writing in a diary? George Davis (leaving Lenya with a German husband buried in America, and an American buried in Germany); Robert Kurka (teaching a lesson to his colleagues); Mike Todd (as spectacularly as his life); W. C. Handy (the evening sun *went down*, if you'll pardon the expression); a Greek-tragedy murder in the family of Lana Turner (she was always a girl-of-the-heart with whom I closely identified). Finally our precious Marie Blanche de Polignac, yes finally (thus ending an *époque* which cannot be revived in this lifetime). Loneliest and nearest was Oscar, though too distant for me to write it now with feeling. In my own ever-increasing interspatial transports how often do I ask why we spend money to keep ourselves alive (buying teeth and doctor bills and cabbages) when it's easier to kill ourselves? The child's revenge of dying gave Oscar the courage of his convictions. And yet I loved him. When I can't sleep I think on movie stars. The presence of beloved parents prevents suicide. Yet some of me died with Oscar: the part he invented through need, and owned.

Elliott Stein writes from Paris of sailors with machine guns pointing from trucks, and war again, or still, seems whizzing around with wings so vast that even the sunniest of these first hot days which make the city streets steam with sex are clouded with the perpetual and necessary hangover, and I go "on the wagon" only to better prepare myself for the next drinking bout—the sooner the better. I miss France to a point of anguish, but through that American sense of *place* (not to mention lack of funds) I remain. The winter's accomplishments (and my sister Rosemary is pregnant for the *fifth* time: it will be born in July) have by-passed my own personality, making me, to an extent, a public figure remote from myself. We can make few generalities on how a composer should live. But don't I know how correct is Waugh, who says that Charm "spots and kills anything it touches. It kills love; it kills art. . . ."

Today I'm as sweet as a violet cream pie, and tonight with the bitchiness of liquor I can spout the aggressively self-assured nastiness which, like Mr. Hyde, good doers must possess. But I've aimed it badly, and seldom in my work. Often composers compose like what they think they are not. Look at the uncomplicatedly sensitive but basically joyous work of David Diamond during his flagrantly disordered war years, and now that he's stabilized in a Florentine villa his music's grown knotty, complex and sad. Observe Marc Blitzstein, whose private ways are circumspect, even to mystery, yet whose music's direct, earthy, of the body. Or myself, who say and show all anywhere while notating sounds repressed and puritan as hymns. Still I know my origins even if I may see influences less objectively than an outsider. *"Je méprise les fils qui rougissent de ressembler à leur*

père," says Poulenc. I always prefer the movies, and anything I
do which is not "me," is still "me" since it's *I* doing it, and we
know that consistency's the hobgoblin of etc. . . .

That question of *influence* is elusive. Composers are always
being asked about it. Yet more interesting than their knowledge
is their ignorance concerning those outer rays that blast them.
When I first arrived in Paris, it was with embarrassment that I
showed my little pieces to everyone, feeling those pieces to be too
outrageously French, too lush, too self-indulgent. Yet Poulenc
exclaimed (as did Sauguet, Boulanger, Milhaud), "Let yourself
go! Why so careful, so Nordic, so Protestant, so unsensual?" Of
course, what even the greatest artist expresses is nothing compared to what he represses. . . . The question of *style* is even
more elusive. Sam Barber, for instance, has no truly identifiable
musical syntax, yet he has nonetheless identifiably influenced
our Charles Turner. Still, Charles' music (at its best) is his
own—though nobody can tell you why.

Last winter's accomplishments: yes, Ormandy played my
piece, and Mitropoulos, and I wrote music for Tennessee's play
about a poet eaten alive last summer by children who cut him
apart with tin cans. Success and establishment, like education,
are cumulative, and for a composer it's never financial, while
Tennessee with all his acclaim never sees a minute's rest and is
given to public confession now. As for Mr. Inge, he's shown me
a libretto about a sodomite undertaker who is required to em-
balm, on stage, the person dearest to his heart.

How could I not be discouraged about librettos, at least for a
while, after last month's ignominious failure of *The Robbers?*
The production was an outrage, with the three actors looking
less Chaucerian than like Jesse James, Leslie Howard, and
Harpo Marx. To add insult to injury, it was co-billed with Rieti's
The Pet Shop (renamed "Amelia Goes to the Dogs" by Elliott
Stein) which received all the praise from *les petits amis.* The
damage of "charm" again, but for once I am not the sinner.

▼▼▼

June

For weeks, for weeks now, in this heat, I have been just staring around this room or out the window which has grown so full of leaves I can't see up to the sky. Or drinking heavily three days out of seven, spending the intervening hours recuperating in nervous sleep. Or waiting for letters from Europe which don't come, or for the right person to make the phone ring (it doesn't). Steambaths are time-consuming and expensive, but I spend and consume. Certainly I do not work (except a few songs for *The Ticklish Acrobat*), just gaze at the window and cry and cherish my tears like a lady her diamonds. To sum it up: today it's June and I've no summer plans, no money, nothing to work on, no love; too much liquor and leisure, too much sleep, and too much worried humidity all over the whole world's sky. I'm thirty-four and waiting: it isn't easy.

The dark will always have it over the light. Around 4 A.M. The day is no longer long enough to drink in. The proof: I'm still able to write it.

▼ ▼ ▼

Well, Nell Tangeman and I've been going to A.A. meetings now for three days, and will continue until I go home to Philadelphia for the 4th of July when Rosemary will have her fifth child. Certainly nothing can be said against their logic: I've thought the same for years and don't want to spend, without help, *all* the rest of my life in that shadow wet with unknown bleeding. But . . . I don't know. I'm not a "group type" (many say that) and do not wish to be *absorbed*. I'm used to being the *only one* at the party, and falling in with a communal plan is a worse change for shyness than going alone onto a long wagon. I'm hell at a party, but heaven on stage. We'll see, I'll give it some chance. Because God knows I'm bored with the boredom of Monday's gin and I don't interest myself anymore. Liquor's black magic, and I'm a mortal with no talent for combating sorcery. My "fabulous life" which astounds so many is now a heap of tedium, and the fatigued wrinkles of my forehead make a drunken demonstration even less dignified than in my earlier youth. And I *do* care, in spite of all the "slips." I care more than all the beat and cool epochs.

Music is seen and not heard by them. Every time the curtain goes up on *Suddenly Last Summer* Bobby Soule's set receives applause but no one ever knows there's music. The surrealists had no ears and so banned music; the new generation uses its ear as a phallus, and is violent only in its lack of violence. Had I been born just four years later I might have fallen into this age which takes the atom bomb for granted (I'm told that even the moon—that dreary suburb—is being prospected only as a military base) and lacks all curiosity; as it is, I remain romantic, liking excess, worrying still on waking up, a broken boy.

Wilhelm Reich is dead also. The times advance with always more *embêtements sans poésie* (as Philippe Erlanger says), and some grow sterile before dying. Last night we saw *The Goddess*, for which Virgil's music is a flaw. His defenses are more brilliant than what he defends. Some people are easy, some hard, to talk to. Virgil talks at and of or through, not to you. But monologuists are better than those who just wait like lumps. A successful conversation is as importantly difficult as a working love affair. Aaron attends, Marc shares, Morris ploughs on, Tennessee stagnates, Marie Laure declaims, Virgil pontificates, but Latouche knew the art more congenially than any. I want to be enveloped (the better to blind by closeness and gobble up), and have no need to envelop; am also a nomad—the faithful nomad —grinding teeth and chewing nails, both of which are now impossible. Our friends do reform. My favorite Heddy over in Paris, now all slim and remarried, no longer tells of orgies and new bars but speaks instead of the fluctuating price of cauliflower. *Oui, je te pardonne. Mais seras-tu jamais réconcilié au fait qu'en essayant de m'aimer tu avais découvert quelque chose en toi que tu aurais préféré ignorer?*

I could no more dare make an authentic list of loves than a total list of *cuites*. Europe is away from my life. And Maggy Teyte and Zorina are (or *were,* a few years back) the cultured American's idea of a Frenchwoman, unrealistic as Fifi d'Orsay, or as we think Beckett (whom I hate) or Ionesco are French. Small wonder that that moon is sought just by soldiers. We are unclear on our nationalities. Yes, conversations are a chore, and as we grow on the efforts of a diary are increasingly tedious.

▼▼▼

> . . . *that doom of genius—the individual's powerlessness in the face of his own powers.*
>
> **—ISAK DINESEN**

The compulsion to compose was with me, until the age of about twenty-eight, as intense as the compulsion to drink—and I was helpless before both: music flowed out of my body like a sweet but slightly sick liquid, and liquor flowed back into it during increasingly frequent periods of *violent relaxation.* This all began in earliest childhood, for both the alcoholic and the creator are latent in the personality long before the first drinks. But today I have much less a *need* to compose than to be appreciated through my composition. I know of what I'm capable, so the muse becomes less significant than the goal. Excessive drinking is a sign of "immaturity," yet the fairyland of youth is the one thing, if when lost, loses the artist. Drinking is childish, creative activity childlike. These two qualities are similar only as black to white and must never be confused.

▼▼▼

Summer feels finally here; we've had no spring, just a long mild winter during which there were flashes of summer (not spring) showing the way Mrs. Depencier (our fifth grade teacher)'s silver blouse used to shine through her slashed sleeves twenty-four years ago when our minds were less on the black-

board than on the sound of a Good Humor wagon through the
math class window coming with the first odors of forsythia and
roses and the first fragrance of young boys and girls. This I
mention because yesterday Bruce Phemister and Charles Mather
came to dine with me on Thirteenth Street and we literally
wallowed back with giggles to mutual recollection of our communal nursery school in Chicago. Then Bill Flanagan gave a
debtor's party for a few composers and nobody got drunk (even
Mark Bucci and Lockrem Johnson) because I've been in A.A.
for five days (tonight I'll go to still another meeting with Bill
I., who's been in for ten years).

Summer feels finally here but yes, those announcing flashes
were showing as far back as March 1st when at Larry Rivers' I
sat for the portrait which was ultimately rejected as a music
cover because Mr. Hinrichsen thought the fingerprints looked
grimy (which they did, but they were part of the picture). So
the August winds of March floated through the rooms as I sat
face to face with Larry whose large sketch pad was upon his
knees spread wide apart and my eyes *had* to concentrate upon
this zone while I wondered how can all those rumored drinks
and pills allow him nevertheless to get up and paint compul-
sively through the day as I used to do but do no more!

With the wind of real Augusts I used to walk with thin
Nancy Mitford in those endless mountains behind Hyères between goat bells and sundowns, while today I can't I can't I can't
go back to France. The murderous vain dumbness of our strong
new scary world makes an ever-huger moral distance between
here and there in space and time; there are not poems, but
science, and I'm four years out of my generation; what's the use
now of recalling the snow dancing around the Paris gaslamps or
the summer smell of boys far off? Even longer ago in Morocco
with Guy we drove Yvonne Loriod over to Meknès where in an
old schoolroom she played for us Albéniz. Today she and all the
others, except me, follow their interests with focus (or do I just

think so?); it's recent enough for me still to identify—and I've too much empty leisure. What lasts?

After nine years across the ocean in countries crammed with historic masterpieces, I've returned (for some reason) to where there are none: to mediocrity in high position, to no more true terror or art, just small *ennuis,* science and jealousy. New York streets, an avalanche of realities like rent and taxes and laundry and canned beans and earning a living and dying. At least it's definite now: Lenny Bernstein will do my new Symphony with the Philharmonic next April. How will I wait? and what shall I write and love between now and then? "In the Summer House"? There was a festival for San Antonio on Sullivan Street, a slum proudly ornamented with great electric clover leaves studded with ruby bulbs, and they sold pink-candy-cotton in the undrunken dancing and pinball machines. I liked that! It's summer all over.

▼▼▼

Sauguet says, when I offer to pay the check after our first meal in a restaurant together circa 1949: *"Non! c'est vous qui payerez quand vous sortirez le compositeur de huit ans."*

When, for Ulysses Kay, I judged the B.M.I. competition, there were entries by infant composers whose *métier* was phenomenal. That's just the trouble!

▼▼▼

Bill Connors, at a bleak midwestern roadhouse counter, asks for a hamburger. The waiter yells the order through the kitchen porthole, then goes immediately *himself* to prepare it. No one else is in sight.

In the New York autumn of 1946 I made these entries in this diary:

No one is in sight. This three-day phrase of willed waste was climaxed and can be temporarily dismissed. Rolled and beaten seven times this month, and room robbed twice. If only I could be generous of myself. But when my madness reaches a pitch the nastiness is highest and my shyness seems coldness; when I manage no responsibilities and don't write any music then the total stink of my character becomes insupportable to the nose of the whole city. Picking my nose this morning was like applying a small sharp shovel to a shredded velvet carpet. The visitor didn't mind —even gave *me* a dollar, longshoreman from Jersey. David says my tastes are masochistic—but even the cruelest need loving. I have a half a bottle of Calvert's left, but as usual I spent all my money again. I'll stop drinking now for a few days to finish my organ piece for Paul.

Yes yes, it's come to that. Nothing—sex, nothing is so important as alcohol. And yet returning here alone I sit inert. How I envy. How I envy. And overcome this hideous shyness drinking, drinking.

I confess that when I contemplate suicide as I do daily there's an element of sour grapes. I don't know why I want to. Don't know why. I've been drinking every night for a week. All I want is to cry. I'm jealous and dishonest. If I don't get laid soon I'll collapse. Yet I won't allow it. Don't like people, really. When I go out tonight I don't care if I come back dead.

Was interrupted (at 3 A.M.) because of Eddie's arrival directly after the soldier left. As for returning dead, of course I didn't, but with Alfonso Ossorio we all went to hear Billie Holiday who came to drink stingers at our table and I went down on her in front of everyone because of her extravagant beauty and because she smells like a Catholic church, not perfume but incense. But I only toyed with her legs, for in that shallow grandeur is an austere intimacy. I find Alfonso charming.

So of course I hinted all my troubles to M. and she is worried. Having been raging for over two-thirds of the past three weeks I've nearly lost my face. To reassure the family I say that I shall discipline myself without the aid

of an analyst. God but we are truly of one blood. M. and
I may be self-indulgent but that doesn't make a personal
world seem less cruel. In phenomenal promiscuity (during
which there's certainly never been realized "the function
of the orgasm") which is sublimated to alcohol, am I re-
treating from love or doubts of talent?

This evening Janet Lauren did two of my songs on her
program. I was moved. Paul Goodman was here and com-
forted me. Jim O'M. just went home, wouldn't come in. I
can't formalize or write or write or write!!! Yesterday was
lost.

Tomorrow Grace and I will go to the dance class. Tonight I must stay home, and alone. And read *Dead Souls*.
How long, O Lord?

▼▼▼

> *And in those days shall men seek
> death, and shall not find it; and shall
> desire to die, and death shall flee from
> them.*
> —REVELATION 9:6

How long—was thirteen years.

At fourteen my first liquor was tasted with friends as an
experimental joke, but doubtless I had the liquory temperament
(or disposition) long before. Being a younger-brother who from
the start was never discouraged in his talent, I dearly loved my
entire family. Still do. We were Quakers of the intellectual
rather than the puritanical variety. Nevertheless, the Friends
Meeting (which in form and content is not dissimilar to A.A.)
lacked an immediate poetry which I later sensed in the silver
incense of a Catholic mass, eventually in musical composition,
and finally in rye whisky. But Catholicism was forbidden:
Quakers inspire restraint which, in my case, was manifested in
shyness.

I loved those first drinks. And although the gaudily imagina-
tive and experimental set in which I moved drank a good deal, I

needed more. Of the "upper-middle-class" with few financial worries, by eighteen I was already a "problem drinker" without realizing it. Never a social drinker unless social can be called forcing friends to stay out all night. Never a morning drinker, unless morning drink can be called the one taken at noon just before going to bed. Never a lone drinker, unless alone can be called the last one in the bar. Sometimes I'd have a first drink alone (I've never taken only one), but its taste brought desire for company and I'd call friends, or go out to *find* friends, to have *fun*, the fun that was later to become frightened boredom, a soured magic. Any friend will do: an addict spends years of melancholy obliteration with people inferior to himself: an intellectual half-nourished on garbage which shames him the next day.

During college the drinking was periodic: exaggerated affectionate weekend binges. At the same time I was passionate about music, and like most young creators would forget myself in work for fourteen hours a day. Because I have never believed in (or at least been able to practice) moderation, today still, and probably always, I do all to excess, am hooked on work. On the wagon I feel *immoderately sober*, never wanting the poison of liquor to infect the now-purified system. . . . At sixteen, when still living at home, I used to have acquaintances phone my parents at 5 A.M. to say I wouldn't be back that night, and would end up in vague hotels. I drank to be grown-up—and the word *alcoholic* had a ring of glamour; I wanted any and all to know I drank: it was "interesting," romantic, to be a lush! Not for years did the lying begin, and I would invent a cold to avoid appointments, instead of admitting to the hangover of which I was formerly so proud.

I am thirty-four. Drinking has occupied two-thirds of my life, and already a combined total of several wet years, has, in a way, been effaced from memory. How did I ever get all that work done? Yet professional success began quite early; and the reputation, which is generally odious, of most drunks was, in my case, one of eccentricity, since artists are conceded to be unmanageable. And when tight I was able to overcome the heavy natural timidity and carnal inhibition which I still retain.

But in my early twenties inordinant rationalizations (which only other drinkers can fathom), procrastinations, undependability, irresponsible reputation, ever-increasing hangovers drenched in self-pity and remorse, all converged in a plot against me, and, to preserve sanity (and also due to an innate sense of order and well-developed ego) I began this diary devoted in part to musical notions, in part to alcoholic reporting on hallucinations and all they imply. Now the *word*, once written, is infallible to the gullible, and I felt, with depressed reasoning, that I could allow anything so long as it was in systematic narration. This started a period of self-indulgence maintained here ever since.

I was inclined usually to write mainly when sad, omitting expanses when reasonably happy or too busy to report my slips. Nevertheless in rereading I am touched by the weight of oppression through the years: how many hundred times did I move in an unremembered dream from party to bar, and room to room, falling, collecting unaccountable scars, playing the fool and confusing the days, wetting the bed and awakening on pillows caked with vomit, hand too shaky to work, tongue bitten like a sponge, character too humiliated (in moments of sobriety) to look anyone in the eye! Work and play became separate as Jekyll and Hyde, and I learned to divorce drink completely from music. Sometimes after a week's carelessness I returned home to find my talent stifled, like a canary lying in the cage dead of hunger. Blackouts so-called seemed less and less amusing, would awaken in beds of strangers, any age or creed or sex, monsters miles from home. The glamorous taste and miraculous effect of the first drinks taken in respectable company would lead deep into evenings of dubious encounter when I'd swallow anything, mix gin with rum, beer with wine, whiskies with each other, averaging twenty-five a night. But not all nights. I was never hospitalized, never had D.T.'s. Despite an enormous capacity I always *showed*

my drinking, though far back in the brain perhaps there lurked a
secret ordered lucity.

In 1947, at the suggestion of friends and in acceptance of the
then-cultural vogue, I began psychoanalysis, heavy Freudian
sessions thrice a week for a year. It's hard to know if this helped;
I'd ostensibly gone to be rid of causes, and though I had occasion
to speak of only myself and adventured deep into the ever-
widening cave of the heart, I did not amend my pattern in
practice. It was always easier to give "shocking details" to close
friends than to the doctor. After a year I was wiser maybe, but
can one know if the couch or just living was the means? At any
rate I stopped analysis abruptly in 1948.

Because I won a cash prize (and instead of wishing to spend
this on the analyst) I decided to go to France as a summer
tourist—but didn't return here to live for eight years! The first of
these years passed in a fairyland which only the "ex-patriot" who
thinks he's shed his origins can understand. I had *not* left behind
in America the infantile qualities of background which made
alcohol appealing. Drinking is contagious and I still grow nervous at being near when I cannot participate. But I swallow
differently, will not do it alone, therefore try to drag all others
down too. The classical pattern: split personality; with the first
sips I grow elated and "witty," then turn to nonphysical belliger-
ence, twisting a knife in a companion's most vulnerable wounds,
finally crumble in a babble of self-pity and obliteration of
unhealthy sleep, awakening twelve hours later in aching remorse
to find the typewriter stolen and blood on the bathroom floor.

I have two needs—to compose, and to drink. These comprise
good and evil, white and black, high and low, agreeable responsibility and total perdition; they are intermingled and at swords'
points; conceivably one could not exist without the other—but
the conflict (and the possibility that it may always be present)
saddens me.

In Morocco from 1949 to 1952 I abstained, partly for love and
the routine of work, but also because geographically the country

is not given to the bar life of Anglo-Saxons. Without, therefore, the possibility of drunken adventure with other drunken adventurers I remained under control and accomplished a great deal during this happiest period. On intermittent trips to Paris, however, I made up for lost time, and would then return to Fez with a sense of having again wasted myself in gratuitous binges. As though the ways of our world did not punish us sufficiently for us not to add a new self-punishment! "Is my flesh of brass?" said Job. Yet we continue. Yes, I am thirty-four, but still for nearly twenty years I have drunk to stop time, retarding myself to a simpler speed. One by one I nervously saw most drinking friends amend their adolescent habits, shape themselves into what's called the *normal* life; "nervously," I say, and vaguely surprised, for at the start, just as everyone on earth was a composer like myself, I also casually assumed that everyone had a liquor problem. Only in later years did I feel isolated or individual. It's not that I need to be understood, but I need *not* to be misunderstood. "What a pity," they said, "that nice talented boy willfully destroying all God gave him!"

Yes, certain geographies do not lend themselves to contagions of drink. I have been drunk in Italy, but only with Americans: that country's temperament is not alcoholized. Oh, to invent a land within, which could withstand the insane rationalizing of the alcoholic who feels his imminent fall! Oh, the desire for cleanliness that comes after drinking: you even wash the soap.

The joys of a clear morning head are preferable to weeks when knowingly I didn't bathe, masochistic netherland of sweat, anonymous hotel rooms, hotel rooms where heart and bed seemed bursting with urine, bleeding and blasting through my anvil head. Could I force myself to do sober what was avoided when drunk? I accept the sterile abyss behind, but the prospect of being unable to plan because of similar abysses stretching (half-voluntarily) until I die could cause a suicide today. No man's an island and half my life's been lived; liquory joys have long evaporated, yet I crazily persist, trying to *swallow myself into the past.* And hide it. And the mocker's mocked. And deathly sick of the make-believe hangover–sexuality when only the body is present. And having written this, and all this through the years, knowing, hating, I am still capable of going out now and getting blind drunk. One must have the conviction that alcohol is negative in order to give it up. I'm not convinced.

PART 8

New York and New England
Summer–Autumn 1958

Rien que cette jeunesse
qui fuit devant la vie.

—ELUARD

At 1:30 A.M., back in the New York of May 29, 1947, my purple ideas on sound were as follows:

Music is the greatest art, the only one which removes us utterly from Earth. Other mediums do it partially but none so completely—that is, for a long enough period to instill at least a temporary change. Music puts us where daily things (living or inanimate) are not. Painting removes us only to another worldly place, another position from where we see objects or landscapes, not with new eyes (naturally) but from new angles. The validity of an art's strength is judged by its magnitude of transport (i.e., does it *send* us). Others try to incorporate into their expression the necessarily abstract impulses found solely in music, for it is toward music which they involuntarily aspire. Painting enlarges scope, literature renovates psychology, but both refer to the finite. They can be eternal, but music alone is infinite. Science excites romantic contemplation on other eternities, dance inspires our most antique catharsis; but definitely these are never all abstract, and total abstraction artificially produced is the nearest thing to sense-genius. The nearest thing to music is mathematics, they say, but also the farthest in that mathematicians are not concerned with exciting our emotions. (Musicians can add and subtract pretty well, and mathematicians like to play in string quartets. That's about as far as it goes.)

Enjoyment I cannot conclude from atonality in music or surrealism in letters. I like surrealist paintings and movies, and these mediums in employing expressionism I like (the latter would correspond to atonality). I think it is because dream, or nonconscious, symbols (surrealism being psychoanalytic) are essentially visual, and hence more convincing in painting, which can separate comic or tragic variations in form and bright color, than in poems, which put into words that which in this case is not spoken. Expressionism is a detailed re-depiction of basic sensations (ordinary objects become emotional experiences), so music could of course never express this—not being concerned with objects—whereas in poem or piece of art such as *Caligari* it is successful. Atonality, then, by this definition, cannot work. But many atonal compositions (12-tone or otherwise) are certainly convincing and beautiful. This is because their core is tonal, and they are expressionist only in that the whole is made of many segments.

Today I'm not clear what I was driving at. But I am clear about the only trouble with Milton Babbitt being that he still takes music seriously. As though it mattered! Still, if he's going to be serious at least he should be consistent. In his recent article he not surprisingly gives the impression that whoever doesn't think as he does doesn't exist. But quite surprisingly he illogically equates music with mathematics by suggesting that a concert audience should be as formally equipped as an audience at a lecture about advanced mathematics, as if science weren't a means to an end, and art an end in itself. They all speak of progress, of evolution, as though these terms were more inevitably applicable to a healthy musical growth than to a cancer.

▼▼▼

Summertime in a great city and a damp musky summer *entrejambes* stimulating fragrance sets my expectant nerves on edge but I never give in. I could almost enjoy the relief of suffering again: it's been long and living's drab without it. One does, and doesn't, grow out of the habit. Looking gold as a peach and

fragile as a fawn, without knowing how to *give*, though ripe for
midsummer orgies with soldiers as in those first war years. If my
enthusiasm for work has grown blasé, could a new intimate body
in love still let me share Kepler's exhilaration when, after 6,000
years, he found the solar system's movement like a labyrinth of
silvery veins and vessels and blood color of jet, platinum, and
cobalt?

A composer isn't necessarily profounder than "real" people,
but what profundity he does have he necessarily communicates.

▼▼▼

Tomorrow I hope to clinch the rights for *Mamba's Daughters*
with Audrey Wood and Dorothy Heyward. But if I *do*, then I'll
have to write it, and (for the record) I've been drinking stupidly
again and feel uninspired. Despite my complaints do I really
want love? The fussy order of my habits keeps everything at
arm's length. Day after day of heat and rain has brought insects
to Manhattan, and I sleep badly. Because abstinence through
A.A. has been an endurance contest and not a state of grace.

▼▼▼

When he sees a beauty in the street, Norris Embry says (in
parody of an A.A. slogan): "There with the grace of God go I."

If I abandon alcohol, what will become of that dear obstreper-
ous kid I've been taking out on a leash for years? I've never made
a clean break with another person, much less with myself.

Have been rereading my diaries: eleven, twelve, thirteen
years ago was the same drunken slobber about the overwhelm-
ingness of liquor as a beloved in this life. What does not happen
to me is my own fault. Another love will be resignation, an event
impossible to evade. But sentiment, like history, does not exist
while it is being made.

Living by formula if not by order, yet suffering daily from
someone new never seen. Those first diaries showed a world
detachment much more *accusé* than today.

Like Roosevelt I will always have friends, though my life's seemed scandalous to some, and a total freedom for work which has never "paid."

Stockyards are concentration camps, butchers are undertakers. It's exciting. A funeral in the treetops.

▼▼▼

Spray Beach. So here I am at a Jersey shore hotel with parents and two nephews for a few days of sunlight and a hair-raising glimpse of Atlantic City. A little bored, it's not unpleasant. I love hotel rooms anywhere in the world: Oran, Santa Marguerita (a year ago), or Germany. Concrete worries are only that the rent's too high, and how will I practically reconcile the joys of unemployment insurance to a month's absence in Peterborough during September?

▼▼▼

Already at fourteen I was anxious about rum cake, or sherry in soup. (*When* will they pass a third round of drinks, O Lord?!) In the freedom of sobriety I grow nostalgic for my prison of the past. I, too, thought I was insane. Consummation can come to the hysterical approach.

▼▼▼

Gertrude Stein writes a French English. Julien Green an English French. Hence the disturbing appeal of their styles. Because who before has ever used Gallic wit and compression successfully in an Anglo-Saxon tongue? or written of miserly Protestant small-town American old maids in the sensual Latin language?

▼▼▼

A plague of children. NO LOITERING. The importance of odor. The ecstasy of the armpit, the right crotch, the loved human breath, fragrance of one's own knee in the sunlight (smell of the sun), or of your best friend's hair.

▼▼▼

Still in the evening New Jersey lobby and about me radios, the *Saturday Evening Post,* Scrabble players, a defunct sunset, etc.

Again A.A. I also cannot sleep and grow irritable at the time of the full moon. The star pupils of our meeting are Charlie Jackson and Bill I. (A month ago, on finding himself alone with me, he jumped into my lap like a Saint Bernard imagining himself a Pomeranian.) At the "closed group sessions" long hours can be spent on how to alleviate melancholia. But this ain't an "alcoholic question" (better stated: how do we avoid *drinking* when depressed or elated?). As Inge justly quotes: "To know life is to know conflict," and the soberest teetotalers can be suicides. At least after two new weeks of sobriety my fantasies are not of golden martinis floating through the sky, but of fudge sundaes or cherry-cheese pie. . . . After the meeting, cake, soft drinks and coffee are served, with a special late-late coffee hour at the nearest Schrafft's. Standard classic slogan: One drink is too many and forty aren't enough. Jay Harrison suggests that the meanest man of the year would be he who spikes the punch at an A.A. meeting! Meanwhile we all grow fat on milkshakes.

▼▼▼

Plan a study on lawless misdemeanors in the Old Testament, and name it "Go Down Moses."

I came to pray and remained to scoff. In spite of nineteen completely sober days, some mornings I still wake up thinking "hangover"; my relief's a clear wind. On correct calculation I have, between the first of the year and June 23rd, been drunk forty-six times (or an average of twice a week), and four times since my first A.A. meeting June 25th.

A nonalcoholic takes a drink or three or sometimes even gets drunk without worrying much about it. But I think and think and think and think. Normal responses which most *living people* take for granted have now for me a new unfearful significance and a sort of charmed open joy: mornings with a clean head, grass and water, a shopkeeper's smile, work without fright. Nor do I even consider its continuation.

I am wrong to say a drunkard's only a drunkard when he's drunk. Alcoholism is a state of mind which can continue even after years of sobriety. A thought of wine can be as sap to a rose or maple. Loud lamenting on sterility soon makes me potent, silent. Suddenly I'm writing four orchestral poems at once: *Eagles, Pilgrims,* a *Chaconne,* an Overture (which was to have been for *Mamba's Daughters*).

▼▼▼

The end of a beginning. It is 2 A.M. Starting the 27th day of new sobriety.

For how long have I been thinking All's contained in me? It's the afternoon of my 35th year when I admit that, if I am of our world, so then are the subtle inventions of my dreaming from the flesh or dust or faint recall of it. If the molecules of my imagination are part of the solar system, did they exist before my birth awaiting my organization? or were they contained in order even then? I wrote that I "knew all about life except how to live it." It's difficult to believe that, although an alcoholic personality is formed quite early, a solution for its outlet can be discovered before puberty. (If Utrillo was hospitalized at ten it must have been for malnutrition and the wine that's in all French families.) The full moon prevents sleep. The saint in hell. "Old-fashioned" in music is self-imitation; the *new* is outmoded with Billie Holiday: her oldest records remain the truest. Black-male.

▼▼▼

In December of 1952 while thinking and sitting alone in my ninth-floor room at the Chelsea Hotel in the rain around 2 A.M.,

I passed the most peculiar moment of my life without action or décor. What else can be said? Because a strange sensation may not be notated and still remain strange. But later, far down in the street I heard the automobiles driving by, driving by in the rain and one of them skidded, then drove on. Where, at this minute, is that car's driver? Where was I? Where will I be in ten minutes? Creation is the recall of something which never occurred.

False pretenses? *True* pretenses!

▼▼▼

Miss Marva Torture. The violent sea storms which have been raging around here are officially given girls' names: Hurricane Daisy, Hurricane Cleo, etc. At Schrafft's is a confection called Amber Mist. Like female impersonators others are: Heather Burns, Pleasant Change, Sylvia Sorrows, Sandra September, Sally You, Witch Craft, Hanna Henna, Miss April Friday. And a new perfume called Get Her. Miss January Summer, Miss Arabella Fantasy, and Miss Fern Sherbet. A massacre of mascara. Her ideal dream—*To Be Fucked by the Unknown Soldier*.

▼▼▼

Today I have been five weeks "dry." On Labor Day, I leave by plane for a whole September of work at the MacDowell Colony. I've sublet for $135 this apartment in the building where twelve years ago Kubly lived twice the size for half the price. Yes, our living is circular. Being obliged to forego the $45 weekly unemployment insurance, I hope to resume it in October.

▼▼▼

Peterborough, N.H. September, 1958
The leaves, the cleanliness, the cool sun, the steeples. I can't believe it! Not since childhood have we been here. Our living *is* circular.

▼▼▼

Begin article (or program notes, or something) with Yeats' quote: ". . . those dying generations at their song." *Making Pieces Today* . . . Anyone goes nowhere. But a painter's blood drips precision and his weakest canvas glows a healthy red. Etc.

End: An artist should think he is able for all. Though nobody goes everywhere. I'm thirty-four. For twenty years I've had an "alcoholic problem." Today a group therapy helps battle compulsion. Has anything been lost or repaired, after or before? The artist's Bad is as good as his Good if not too many dishes are smashed in domestic quarrels.

Picasso: Every artist is half man and half woman, and the woman is usually insupportable.

▼▼▼

Harp, Flute—Boys, boys
Flute, Cello—Boys, girls
Fruit Jello—Girls, boys
Cello, Harp—Girls, boys (for parties)
Harp, Flute, Cello—Boy!

▼▼▼

The metronomic value of my normal heartbeat is 74½.

▼▼▼

I love profoundly, and always have, both parents. And used to be shy. Logic helps to overcome it.

▼▼▼

Question: Do you like Keats? Answer: I don't know what they are. (Brahms and Yeats may also be used.)

▼▼▼

She combs her hair, not brushes it. Like painting a jewel, not polishing.

▼▼▼

This morning Ralph Shapey came out with the old romantic banality that the basic instinct is fear, birth a traumatic shock. But *why*? What of the frisking newborn colt? Or the throbbing cocoon from which a near-finished butterfly strives to emerge, a tiny rainbow, and fly far off? Or the mass of eggs bursting together into the yellow contentment of perfect chicks? Maybe the infant makes a screech of joy from his successful effort to escape the black unfragrant womb. In all the universe natural life seeks light. The joys of being born. The joys of birth. The silence of real luxury. The virtues of idleness.

▼▼▼

Blaze of change in the healthy green and ill red of fall each morning as I trot to my quiet studio for long hours' work, and the routine of each day is unchanged, offers no problems. A luxury prison. The necessary Prison of Creation. The Mac-Dowell Colony. It will soon be a year since I last left Europe.

Here in New Hampshire I'm up every morning before eight —which is a good three and a half hours earlier than for years I've been rising in the city. When I return to New York in October I will have accomplished a great deal: in eleven days I've already finished *Pilgrims* (based on *Le Voyageur sur la Terre*, the most disturbing story I know) and am well into the orchestration of *Eagles*. There are few distractions—just a nonsexual routine. If there are no "possibilities," neither are there temptations, so one thinks of other things with evenings passed in the unstimulating though pleasant enough company of "average scholars," mostly playing Chinese checkers with Louise Talma. It is the abstinent productive countryfied solitary cooling time of year when one "takes stock." Suddenly, after a decade and a half of obsessed song writing I find the human voice hateful and opera silly: singing is bastard, pitched words super-fluous, and I want to write just music with titles. This is what I feel while building the morning fire in my isolated studio and

smelling clearer than yesterday those fires of olive wood on
winter days in Fez as I orchestrated the First Symphony nine
years ago. And I've never liked anything Spanish: zarzuelas,
black enthusiasm, castanets, the corrida. Why? My nephew
Paul, age five, asks: "Are you a grown-up?" How do I answer?

▼▼▼

The surrealists were positively anti-music. In fact the only
literary movement ever to take up music is our own America's
"cool generation" and it's done it all lazily and wrong.

▼▼▼

Woolcott Gibbs, Vaughan Williams, and Florent Schmitt
have just died.

▼▼▼

I know more people than anyone and, what's more, they
believe what I say, which is always surprising since I never say
what I mean and up here they don't dig my number, which is
pince-sans-rire and "I love the movies more than anything"
though I've overcome my timidity through years of persevering
logic, and other people are dumb too.

▼▼▼

The entire sun belongs to that lizard stretched naked beneath
it there.

▼▼▼

No longer the spoiled child of the Paris years, nor as young as
I used to be. My work must now speak, if not *for*, at least *with*
me. (I couldn't convince Audrey Wood through charm alone!)
When Thomas Mann in 1940 came to lecture of war at North-
western I disguised myself as Tadzio and sat in the front row of
Scott Hall imagining to divert him—without avail. With Bruce
Phemister in grammar school in our unchanged voices we

phoned expensive restaurants commanding rare menus never to
be paid for (that was when I learned of hollandaise sauce), or
from the florist ordered gardenia ships sent C.O.D. to rich
classmates. When Dietrich said "noblesse oblige" that night, my
reaction was: Who does she think she is, Marlene Dietrich?

▼▼▼

Working well: a long fructuous spasm. That's why the diary's
dull. Rain, rain and a state of unrest here because of a strange
series of thefts in the colony studios.

I recall an uneasy breakfast ten years back at five in the afternoon with poor Peter Marchant (dead now, leaving Van
Vechten's biography unfinished) who said that constant carous-
ing had come to make my cheeks look like lard and ashes. Always
in music I overmix colors as I do perfume, flowers. Rain.

Music titles: The Jail of Rain, Invisible Cages, Chaconne on
Drowning, A Quaker Prayer, Homage to Movies, *Le Pardon de
la Mer* (a custom in Brittany).

▼▼▼

The poet always knows where he's going, though he doesn't
always know he knows. He works in showing what he didn't
know he knew.

My romantic defeat is in desiring the role of Innocent Master.
Love without love: the melancholy of masturbation: builds to
nothing.

We think of Death as White Dressed in Black, but dying
foliage takes the color of human health. Why in fall are red
leaves red? Because that season wounds the forest. And I seem to
pass my days in wounding orchestration paper with a razor
blade. . . . My dreams are so real that the pain of daily
awakening is like pulling a scab from the wound of day. The
pain of missing Europe is sometimes unbearable. Yet I can get
up with joy in the early country. My passivity has more power

than your aggression; your action's weaker than my passion; my passivity thicker than your activity.

Moon. The crescent sets fire to platinum trees. The pain of burning logs which take so long to die. Not being a poet by trade I can afford the banalities of nostalgia while smelling back through the years those childhood apples of Oberlin or Yankton, and later of Fez. The nights are already very cold and the days rainy and isolated. New York will be shocking.

▼▼▼

This afternoon during an hour at Esphir Slobodkina's cottage, I painted a picture which turned out to be a cat's face. Now I've always hated cats (being jealous I suppose, because I'm like them, and wise to their crafty ways). This cat is seen inside out, his purple flesh and chartreuse arteries lay bare to the surgeon's knife. But I didn't know what it was until Esphir told me.

▼▼▼

We never really get accustomed to beauty, nor to eccentricity. I learn too quickly, I get the hang of games and trades, and so lose interest in the concentration of perfection (or at least of certain perfections). But we never forget our first step forward though it is followed by an infinite number of identical steps. I can recall the circumstances of each new French word learned, yet I have used them all ten thousand times since. And do not the reflexes of Jean Lafont oblige him, after years of feeding his bulls at night, to recoil before the fiercest, even as I, a novitiate, do? We are never reconciled to beauty, and I am glad to see Marie Laure still clap her hands at what I'd take for granted she takes for granted. What! does the artist pause before the empty canvas, the white page, the blank staff? The beginner doesn't know that this first pause of "where-am-I?" will be forever repeated.

After a dark New England week we are now released from our prison of raindrops. Half of the colonists have already left and I too will next week if Mother and Father come to drive me back. I am always austere.

▼▼▼

The Young are always young, but the Old are young and old, and so the Young have the advantage.

Bees, hornets, wasps, spider webs, gnats, ants, daddy longlegs blur and imprison my reading in the sun. Apparently I once had appeal: I was led to believe and said it myself often enough. I am weathering well: not resignation (which I dreaded) but simply through involuntarily new interests. The pleasures of insanity.

Yes, the leaves by the billions have a stained glass pale orange and pink. And on the 30th (after a month of this sexless and profitable protected pastorale) I return to urban agitations via Boston, where I'll spend twenty-four hours just sight-seeing alone.

▼▼▼

Since tomorrow I leave and time will start again, I'll write a page here while there is still no time. Intoxication. I used to drink because I thought I ought to, though an acceptance in politeness could start off days of oblivion. Yes, I am aware of all the true reasons *why* I drink (as well as the false ones *when* I drink) but knowing them is no prevention. I've been "dry" now for ten weeks, the longest in my life (longest *what?*), though Eleanor before I left New York had "gone" nine months, the length of a pregnancy, which makes her an honest woman. There is no thought of alcohol in the MacDowell Colony because there is no life of either past or future but only a store-house release where the concentration is on forming memory from memories.

▼▼▼

New York, Autumn 1958

Thoughts from Boston: All that can still inhibit me is the living proximity of a myth: the possible lover, the famous poet, the beautiful actress; that is, someone who can *do* something tangible (or changeable) to and for me. So I'm struck dumb.

The museums there showed John Singer Sargeant, the Henry James of pictures. The Harvard campus, alone, early evening and the dormitories begin lightening as the students (nervous from first late classes) return to jerk off. Those varied and vast minorities to which I belong.

Pain of good-bye. Yet I came back a week ago, afraid, inhibited, and broke ten weeks of abstinence built carefully as a web. *Back to unreality,* I like to call it; for when, in New York, are we willing to find five reflective minutes?

▼▼▼

The hideous hours of early evening.

▼▼▼

Yesterday night, after the A.A. meeting, Norris and I visited Eugene [Istomin] who is now *the* "successful pianist." (The pope died as we were talking.) Norris on the one hand, just home from Greece, is more shaken up than ever, needs a lawyer, has no focal point of American ambition. Eugene on the other hand is calm and established, professional and uncreative, rich in the way he wishes. There I lie in the middle: well-launched but without a performance, the envy of many but without a cent, and miracles no longer come (though we get out of only what we put into our miracles). Art, if you'll pardon the expression, is dying: its audience has grown huge while its makers have melted into such tiny specialists that there'll be no miracle here. Certainly our eyes admiring a masterpiece cannot see the same thing as those that looked one hundred or two years ago. As for A.A. its principles don't evade the agreement of my intellect, but it's no easy joke to relinquish live drinking, to become a dead drunk (meaning a *former* drunk). I am Saint Augustine still moaning. Lord, make me good—but not yet! A drunk in the back row complains that women on the wagon grow frigid, to which Ann G. retorts: not frigid, just fussy. There is nobody but people around. I am all reticence or dogma, deaf also, and they don't listen anyway. I said: there is no more connection between a novelist and playwright than between a dancer and an actor. Eleanor says: but didn't Ruby Keeler happily combine the two? She missed the point doubly.

An American composer must live here whether he likes it or not. Whether he knows it or not it is here that his most interesting problems will at least be presented if not solved. Norris (always in trouble) says the Sartrian French agonize in the shadow—not the substance—of the past. Who then are *we* while over there? Hermits in a bird sanctuary? living in nature as though we were it? We aren't.

PART 9

Pennsylvania and New York
Autumn 1958

In some strange way we devalue things as soon as we give utterance to them. We believe we have dived to the uttermost depths of the abyss, and yet when we return to the surface the drop of water on our pallid fingertips no longer resembles the sea from which it came. We think we have discovered a horde of wonderful treasure-trove, yet when we emerge again into the light of day we see that all we have brought back with us is false stones and chips of glass. But for all of this, the treasure goes on glimmering in the darkness unchanged.

—MAETERLINCK

> *In madmen the fascination of the aberrant idea, the fascination of the thing that should not be done, operates by virtue of the same laws that govern expression and the works of art in general.*
>
> —HENRI MICHAUX

The Mescaline House. Although tonight I'm exhausted from the weekend John G. arranged at his house in Crescoe, Pa., so that Paul Bowles and I (and he and a friend Anthony) could have an experiment in mescaline effects, I want nevertheless to note here the sequence of reactions while they're fresh.

Preliminarily let it be said that two exterior elements of preconditioning prejudiced—or at least tainted—my relish of the drug. First is a relation to Paul, who fascinated me from our first meeting in Taxco 1941 (I was sixteen) until our orgy of hashish on Rue de la Harpe in 1949 with Bill Flanagan and Shirley Gabis. I need him to know I exist, that I too am aware of evil (which however I am not in the sense he is). Second is the unheeded warning from Jane F., my A.A. sponsor, about whom I constantly thought.

As to a knowledge of mescaline itself, I'd read Huxley's first book, but felt already experienced in all that detail. But other fanatics, particularly Bill Miller, had so long sung its praises with such determined astonishment that I could no longer wait. They had explained mescaline as neither a soporific nor a stimulant, but a legal nonaddictive device for showing how things are—not how they aren't (as do alcohol, heroin, or the self-imposed dullness of daily living). The pill is theoretically obtainable at any drugstore without prescription, but is now nearly obsolete, its medical function of inciting artificial schizophrenia never having been verified. By diverting us from the constant protective concerns of food and fear, by melting the censorial barriers of conditioning and removing us utterly from ourselves, by chemically lowering the armored instinct of self-preservation, mescaline heightens an awareness of what is about us always but to which we have blinded ourselves in order to live. It deflects from the business of our own death and permits full concentration on the slightest fact of surroundings. Under normal circumstances, perceiving the always present fact is no simple matter, even for the detailed maniac, or the genius who has occasional minutes of illumination which he strives to retain in memory and then preserve in marble. Today, on swallowing a tablet literally anyone can be exposed for hours to a "miracle" which hitherto only an artist or saint had known in scattered moments.

I had heard of this drug's ability to advance us a million years in evolution (or does it, rather, advance us backward to how we reacted in earlier states?), arousing an instant knowledge of true and false, an intuition of the speech of bees and unspoken thoughts, a recognition of color too bright for casual vision, a sense of electrons revolving in steel one trillion times per second, a sound of the live earth breathing into the feet—in short, a conscious observance of the never-still skeleton of our universe: no longer to see "through a glass darkly" but through the night rent by accurate lightning that continues its glare making a plausible world of every raindrop. And I had heard that all this was encountered without loss of control to body or mind, and no hangover! Who would not be tempted?

So I took mescaline, quite unprepared for what was to be thirteen hours of horror.

John drove Paul and me to his country mansion four hours from New York. (Anthony joined us later that night.) After some nourishing meals and a wonderful night's sleep we awoke into the fairest October Sunday one could hope for: acres of personal sky and miles of forest with blue and magenta leaves in total quiet. Europe may have the edge on us in many wonders, but nothing equals America's autumn of which this day was an ideal sample. The house itself was pleasant enough: Cape Cod cottage combined with heathen seraglio heaped to bursting with incongruous objects: stones, pods, Audubon prints, Persian editions, incense, velvet, chains, colors, stuffed animals, and a live female mongrel named Erix. This décor must have been established expressly for the use of mescaline novitiates.

We could have chewed John's dried peyote buttons, which are what the Indian discoverers use and cost seven cents, but as these cause nausea and hallucinations we swallowed instead, precisely at 2:15, the fifteen-dollar pills—although neither button nor pill was advisable for the weak liver of Paul, who was submitting to the experience as to a necessary operation.

For an hour, no effect. Paul and I strolled through the forest to a little river while the others weeded the garden. Then began an agreeable withdrawal as with an overdose of codeine. Things seemed the same (meaning beautiful as they should be right then) but lips grew icy, and face, and finally whole body, and as Paul was shivering we returned to the house. Neither of us had expected physical effects, but they grew worse. Our host and his friend now reappeared with prehistoric grins, and henceforth all came thick and fast.

We were invaded by violent lassitude in which the visual was superclear. John took me to see a rose in the cool sun shuddering with luminous crimson pleasure: a puff of cigarette smoke and the flower recoiled. The cigarette was ludicrous, tasted false. We walked through a wood where trees murmured with reason: each seemed at once male and female embracing itself, arching toward the sky, to live, with ten thousand leaves twittering correctly. All was Life: the sky streaked with ivory veins, the hills breathing, nothing still, everything motion, inhaling, striving, fluttering, speaking delicate wounds. Whole outdoors a labyrinth of hypersensitivity: the sound of sap in the maple's arteries, the emerald chlorophyll throbbing through apples in the grass as I stepped compassionately among them. Nature in her force cares nothing for us except as we unite with her like a "thinking reed," more reed than thought. Mescaline banishes ambition along with vanity; cigarettes taste false because they have no part of living. And while on the verge of knowing the animals' language we have no desire to "write all this down for later." We are Now.

So the effects increased and were not all pleasant. Man-made insertions into this scene were outrageous: a slash of paint on bark, a bridge, strips of barbed wire seemed contradictory as death. Autos on the landscape were ridiculous, even indecent; all human indication was a blotch of blood. Blood everywhere: the wooden fence was a tree skinned alive, and a poplar whose lower branches had been hacked off seemed really to gasp. Nature weeps, and though vegetation is not human we experience the lacerations of fruit or leaf as though they were ours. For all outdoors is flesh, even the wind.

My own physical state became at that point atrocious and I had no sense of touch, my body was glass and fear, and both Paul and I were taken with jitters, chills. Observing the faces of these friends, I saw only varicosed monsters of arteries and teeth. Teeth (and the marks of teeth in food) are the ugliest human possession and the real from the false are instantly perceived. Like cannibals we bite into a stalk of celery. Once back in the house ice became epileptic fire. The shocks continued.

Looking into a Goya reproduction the artist speaks out and

you see through layers to canvas. The three-dimensional photos and advertisements in *Life* magazine scream with the mediocrity of all that's man, and men are vicious sheep, sad and scared. But my own hands were beautiful: a few days ago I had ripped open the cuticle of my thumb: now this small red hole was a great glowing pink marble entrance through which I could gaze into the mechanism of my inner body. I was afraid to turn around, felt menaced from all sides by my companions no longer human—or rather, more human than I, and so ugly. Knives. Everywhere knives and breathing veins. The presence of those kitchen choppers made me want to escape while too heavy on my feet to budge; not the familiar unsteadiness of alcohol for which I am prepared, but a new sluggish lucidity of dope from which there is no turning back. I felt out of control without knowing where to find the safety valve. No blur, it was freezingly clear, a total awareness of the state of unawareness, forced to examine, examine all in novel detail, like it or not, untrained, without order, not understanding pictures which spoke, moving objects, blood on the ceiling, knives, knives. I feared sharpness and being cut or cutting. Outdoors animals screeched, animal night noises all around, the dog looked at us and knew. (Or did she?) Matta's oils bled. My eyes bled. Paul, without feeling it, had a liver attack, his bony hands, luminous green and transparent, clutched at the organ and tore it out as he grinned, his face all molars. Each "normal" experience was now an involuntary experiment of perception. To satisfy this awful energy I drew twenty pictures in five minutes, all of them huge eyes. (John later declared them to be groins.)

Because of how the others looked, I was doubtful about seeing myself since I knew the reflection would be *a truth of flaws* to which I might even be indifferent; yet upstairs in the bathroom mirror I saw no change (except, of course, teeth, always yellow fangs, skeleton bursting out of our mouths, plus a few bemusing wrinkles I'd never admitted), and would have stayed riveted for hours if some flies with monstrous eyes buzzing about the bulb hadn't frightened me. I screamed for help and Paul came up and swatted them. (Poor precious dear sweet brother flies now lying stupidly dead there in the toilet bowl!)

They said my little speech defect had gone. Colors intensify greatly and take a new sense: synthetic dyes are immediately distinguishable from true vegetable tone. Blindfolded, one tells black from white by touch, and after the first frozen shakiness has worn off one finds a certain level of calm on which to examine. Authenticity can, to an extent, be distinguished from fakery, and the painting the artist made from his wife's menstrual blood looks just that. The stars, the whole mass of heaven, take on a bony form where the planets can be *seen* whirling through space at unthinkable speeds and all movement is related to all other movement. The very globe of our world heaves and perspires beneath the feet. My own face seemed unmarked by the eternal qualities of avarice and anguish, etc. John later said it was a *pure* face as opposed to those other filigrees of rings and shadow. Since I am not basically visual, everything I saw was a revelation, but my reaction to music and literature, which normally mean most, were without interest: it was difficult to concentrate on the printed word, and my discernment in music seemed unchanged although the quality of performance is more obvious. (I would like to have heard some of my own with the intention of finding where I may have "conceded," but I doubt I'd have learned much.) Appetite is decreased and meat—especially its odor—is out of the question. For instance, when the dog was given her supper, the smell infected the entire house like an *abattoir*. (Incidentally, I felt no empathy for the dog because, as Michaux points out, dogs haven't any.) If there is a craving it's for oranges, tomatoes, but it's cruel to eat even them, they shriek.

Loss of balance. Sexual impulse reduced to nothing, though certain affection came after fear of being attacked was overcome. I did not want to be left alone with my razor which gleamed on the table like a gypsy crystal—didn't wish to be left alone yet kept leaving the others to find my own boredom of discovery out in the night which also scared me.

For night had fallen now. It was a green doped nightmare in part quite vulgar. Ambition was plain silly. Paul sometimes reverted to babyhood and I grew protective: qualities opposed to our natures. Of the four, Paul appeared the validest human, especially after nightfall (because sin is for darkness). Then Anthony brought me a welcome cup of tea in what I think was the Holy Grail. Outside we examined the heavens, their careless logic, felt Earth's revolving purpose rightly placed and spinning about the neat framework. Then I peed for the first time since morning.

All had been foreseen in that cat's face painted last month at the Colony. There was nothing, nothing pleasant about it. Around nine the effects wore off, thank God, little by little like petals drooping back into place. During the long postmortem I was told my preadolescent erections were inspired uniquely by sado-masochist images. John said my whole nonpleasurable tantrum was because I just couldn't face the truth mescaline offers. Is it the truth? After twenty years of drinking I am less a prophet for alcohol than he for this. At 3 A.M. after thirteen hours of unbroken tension I retired to a battered insomnia relieved only by an unusual nosebleed. I really learned little, though John's pose of sophisticated despair and nineteenth-century refinement was quite dismaying. (He's always struck me, at least in his writing, as the poor man's Paul Bowles—though of course much richer.) I'm already a selfish poet and since childhood have found flaming cities in the porous furrows of a common brick. Any poet has seen this, though perhaps not with such relentlessness, seen the stars fly and grasped their relation, felt the earth revolving, himself carried along through the galaxy like a well-built boat in the sea. I prefer to learn, to hide, in my own Ned way and never to meet them again.

The truth of beauty was evident, certainly, but had to be counterbalanced by the truth of ugliness. There is no shortcut

for paradise, to coin a phrase. Today my eyes ache from having
seen too much. Otherwise there is no hangover, the incident is
finished. This morning (Monday) before returning to New
York we inspected everything again, the trees and skies, the dog,
the velvet. Everything looked exactly the same as under mescaline but also exactly different, without the vibrant hideous
charm: all was, thank God, now quite banal. I recall the episode
as "Dead of Night," a filmed country orgy far off, disagreeably
weird, a fourth-dimensional fever, not forgotten but over, unnecessary surgery, a gash in consciousness and conscience, a slash
in a vacuum, an acrid perfume which had always been around
unsmelled. But I am a nearsighted Norwegian who still knows
that vision is important only to the blind.

▼▼▼

Lions and the sun, two happy fixations. I could wish to be
absorbed, gobbled up in the sunburst of a lion's mane. Drowned
by the sun.

I've never conceded, nor can ever ever accept the world on its
own terms. Because they invent their own rules they avoid the
true challenge, and confound creation with color. I pretend to
enjoy myself but haven't for years. Yet I fool even me.

Rain, dreary, hangover, weary, it continues. Tomorrow I am
thirty-five.

▼▼▼

Today I am thirty-five.

Fifteen years ago I had my first public performance of importance: a Psalm for male chorus with woodwinds, played by Bill
Strickland with the Army Music School in Washington. I was
nineteen. Since then I have written so much vocal music in so
many different forms that suddenly the whole effort appears
shredded by ridicule and now (for the moment at least) I loathe
the human voice, opera's a mockery, songs a profanation. The
end. A.A. gave me a birthday party last night at which I didn't
show up. And Jean Stein (my "fiancée" who'll be married in a

month) gave me pink pajamas from Bergdorf Goodman's.
Uncle David died today. And the Harrisons' second daughter
was born, named Troy Nedda in my honor.

▼▼▼

"Is the bath water hot?" he inquired.

"In a way," she replied.

"And will you go out afterward?" he interrogated.

"There's no place to come back to but home," she retorted.

"Well, did you see Helen today?" he queried.

"Well, in a way," she noncommittalized.

"She *is* very lovely," he exclaimed.

"Vaguely," she proffered.

"Has she been divorced? and did you water the plants?" he
desired to know.

"Sort of," retaliated she.

"Whatever became of Maxine Sullivan?" he mused.

"I wouldn't know," she avowed.

"Do you enjoy Michelangelo?" he suggested.

"Oh, somewhat!" she quipped.

"Well then things are back to normal," he ejaculated.

"Or almost," she alluded.

"Oh! la la! and whoops Bessie!" he sighed.

"Soft gentle pussywillows," shrieked she.

"Time is nearly up," he joked.

"Hardly," she agreed questioningly.

"Is the bath water cool?" he stated, amused but bored.

"Kind of," she asked.

And then he added: "The insanity of innocence is also the
smile of danger."

▼▼▼

The smile of danger. Mescaline. Extreme naïveté is certainly
akin to the one-track mind of madness without the art or crime.
Ignorant of danger I died of joy a thousand times in the Chicago
park of my early teens.

Mescaline: the distortion of accuracy (or vice versa). I'll never be the same again. It functions like the apple of Eden. And I saw death at work in faces, molecules whirling in tables, heard the speech of flowers. There was no place to alight.

Peyote. Today calmly I ask: how does it benefit those plants (99 percent are born to blush untasted) to contain that which may enrich or demolish not only an animal body but a mind? Conversely, could certain flesh produce a corresponding hallucination in certain vegetables? Picture a dahlia raving mad!

▼▼▼

It was the most significant single event of my life. By which I mean: self-contained experience within a specific breath of time. Love, for instance, is a continuum. Nor is marriage an experience, but the preparation for experience. Other events may have been more "important," but less compact, less singular. Nevertheless it is wonderful only in retrospect. Now when passing a meat market with its pink cadavers hooked in the window, or rushing through Times Square in a swarm of apprehensive stares, I say: Thank God I'm not seeing this with mescaline. But on days of pure nature, as with an autumn rainstorm, I wonder nostalgically how those myriad crystals might look if observed through the telescope of our unveiled eye. Or a gigantic microscope. The sky was a naked bulb lighting a concentration camp, an eye that saw all and couldn't shut, the power of lightning that cannot be extinguished, the truth glimpsed by a dying man who cannot expire. Mescaline does for the eye what marihuana does for the nonmusician: helps to dissociate the solos of a jam session. What effect has it on the blind? On lovers? What does love *mean* under it? For it can make us critical but, alas, not creative (though on the surface it would have a specific allure for artists). And lovers are ambitious, whereas with mescaline ambition (i.e., gain) disintegrates.

Which is why the desire to smoke was eliminated as futile, human meanings grew pointless, nature (or an object) represented only itself, what happened was what happened. Eden's apple glowed a warning against exploring the independent inner mind. Nature, ignoring us, lives her own life. All moves. Nothing in the universe is calm. Perhaps an Angel is Stillness. The conscious, stripped of an instinct for self-defense, carries us to a luminous island of innocence.

▼▼▼

Does a person carefully reared in Nature have any need of Art?

Since my mescaline excursion three weeks ago I've read the last chapter of the *récit* by Michaux, who after an overdose six times stronger than "normal" takes the reader into a new plane, and Huxley's second book *Heaven and Hell*. I don't know. As a family the four of us were accustomed to communal nudity. From birth to adolescence I saw my parents and sister nude without thinking twice, and I assumed other families followed similar comportment. Only I, at puberty (for other reasons), covered myself; but even today the rest are as they were. My behavior with persons remains as it was when I met them, i.e., with Paul Bowles today I am again sixteen in Taxco. With someone met a week ago I act a week younger. I have separate personalities (none of which is *me*) for everyone, and with two or more persons I become what I become by rapport with the room's strongest character—or else I go "on stage" (and may be pushed off)—even when both Love and Seniority are present. Tonight, for instance, I have asked Morris, Marc Blitzstein, and Virgil T. to dine (we shall have a sirloin from Esposito's, baked potatoes with a half-pound of butter, salad with thyme, Mother's gorgeous homemade plum jam, ice cream with tangerine sauce, and my niece Mary's cookies). I shall be a child then, until the after-supper guests arrive—a host, nervous, *désintéressé*.

▼▼▼

Joe LeSueur, as everyone knows, is Menotti's secretary now. All day long he hears the maestro composing a new opera in the next room. Gian Carlo emerges for a cup of tea and asks, "Well, Joe, how does it sound?" Joe, at a loss for words: "Well, mmm, it sounds as though something terrible is going to happen." Frank O'Hara later adds: "Something terrible *is* going to happen. He's going to finish it."

▼▼▼

Music I hate: Flamenco, Berlioz, Viennese waltzes. Maggy, who knows I also can't stomach Schweitzer or the blind, proposes a hell wherein the good doctor conducts, throughout eternity, the music of Johann Strauss to which sightless couples dance with Spanish gusto as Hector applauds in my ear.

Last night Lee Hoiby played us his opera which only confirms my new convictions about the overall silliness of the genre. Why bother to sing such exposition as: the chamber pot has disappeared? Dwight Fisk fingered a continual elaborate improvisation as literal background to the text. His music wilted into descriptive padding but was funny because of it. Which is not to denigrate Lee, who's serious in spite of it, and whose talent is singular and necessary. Yet jealously I see these boys, all younger than I, pulling down plump commissions while I go on living with $45 a week—*too lazy to be untrue to myself.* But at least today (and tomorrow?) I am not drinking, am feeling well, not compulsive. Autumn with cold brown rain is here. Indoors it's warm and bright.

▼▼▼

Indian Summer. How many bars have I been thrown out of or not served in? 11,509.

Mescaline. Recognition of the unrecognizable. Unfamiliarity of the familiar. The opposite of a dream. Horror of eternal repetition.

▼▼▼

Last night again I gave a little dinner party with the same menu as Sunday but different guests: Bernie and Bob Holton

with Marvin Levy, and as star Bill Inge. Later came Bill
Flanagan with Edward Albee (whose new play about Bessie
Smith is dedicated to me), and also Kenneth Pitchford with a
poet friend. Such gatherings in my small room are expensive not
only financially but in time and tension since I must not only
cook but keep the conversation going without a drink myself.
However today I've no hangover and there can be fire without
smoke (and when some people die, they just die, and that's the
end of that). Edward's cordial but pointed retort to my conten-
tion that there's been no literary theater for 150 years, is that I
listen for meaning and not for sound. He feels he's been more
influenced by his composer friends than by dramatists, that he
will write a phrase like *"Help!"* or *"I want to go home"* less for
intrinsic meaning than for its rhythm or echo of what comes
before and after. As for Marvin (who one year ago devotedly
helped me furnish this room from the Salvation Army, only to
find the luxuriant bed a seething nest of bedbugs), he is as fond
of opera as we are of the movies, and perhaps we'll find out that
he (being Jewish) retains that grand tragic sense the rest of us
lack. Meanwhile Kenneth's friend, who doesn't know Inge is
Inge, says Inge satisfied needs of this decade (as America's
foremost uncontroversial playwright) but will go out with the
sixties.

This afternoon we're going to play *The Ticklish Acrobat* for
Libby Holman, whom I love and when I grow up I'd like to
marry, and this evening I dine at Jennie Tourel's: a day with the
glamour girls. On seeing Montgomery Clift drunk as he was,
how can I not recall what they all say of me: why? he's young,
famous, talented, rich, handsome? why?—and there's no answer.
To make a work of art does take a certain minimum of happy
concentration. *Maria Golovin* herself is without interest. A
month longer and she could have been.

▼▼▼

Sobriety does not provide (for me, anyway, yet) climaxes,
landmarks. A time span has usually been punctuated by a binge.

Sobriety for the moment lacks contrast and life has stopped at a comma, a vast hesitation, a dull though not unpleasant disappearance of danger. My flesh is willing but the spirit is weak.

Most people aren't drunk most of the time. But: most people don't dream in color most of the time.

▼▼▼

Had a very busy day today: very busy sleeping. The other ME is always on the verge of knocking to get in (or out), and he gets out (or in) with increasing frequency. Sunday after three dry weeks I got drunk and it took me four days to recover from the shock. It was from perversity of tension. Is it "right" to purposely sicken myself? Am I (inversely to what I've always thought) a composer to justify my alcoholism? I wish I could be nice like everyone else. Entire days pass when my only wish is to cry. I will try A.A. again.

▼▼▼

Thanksgiving is gone.

Anything *nuancé* or delicious I might consider notating will be obliterated by a *cuite:* Sunday's was paralyzing. Beginning with a party of heavy martinis for Jean Stein at Ruth and Zachary Scott's (from whom I stole a Persian perfume bottle of apricot crystal) it finished in vomiting bile. Well. Newness is a constant change of mental decor. But Greenwich Village has lost its lights for me.

Sartori is the note G. Write a piece with the calm G (open string of second violins) sounding throughout but which we do not discover until the end. Bombard the G until it's hit. Mescaline again. My picture painted in New Hampshire was a prophecy, not a reflection of the experience. A piano is a tree flayed living with hanging brass veins. The wounds are coated with varnish.

Tyrone Power is dead.

▼▼▼

More Titles:
  Malice in Wonderland
  Emergency Artist
  Gorgeous Numbers (essay on geometry)
  Indecent Proposals
  Certain People
  Sun
  Certain Parks
  Someday the Rain
  Water Music
  Dignified Funerals
  Many Many Movie Magazines
  The Question Remains Unanswered But Is Resolved
  The Answer's Always There But We Never Listen
  Smoke Without Fire

The Ticklish Acrobat. To John Myers, exasperating though he is, most of us owe a lot. Publicly he remains in the background, but it's curious to realize that a decade ago he was New York's chief Renaissance-type promoter for its own sake of the then avant-garde—whatever it was. If George Sanders worked in the *commedia dell' arte* that would be John, glass in hand with swirling cubes, moving unshyly with shrill opinion among the great or the grand, making them (through convincing persuasion or plain annoyance) cough up. It's beside the point now to say that if he never existed we'd have to invent him, or if it weren't him it would have to be someone. It's time to give John Myers his dubious due. Although fidelity is a question of dates and I now feel hampered by John's endorsement (we can't remain eternally beholden for past favors), he was nevertheless directly responsible for my introduction into the *View* milieu; for all my early theater music from Kurt Seligmann's puppet shows of 1945 through Maria Piscator in 1949 to *Suddenly Last Summer* last winter; for Larry Rivers' portrait, and my collaborations with

Herbert Machiz; and for being a friend of music which he really knows nothing about. (But who does?) At the moment he's flattered me and Kenward Elmslie into nearly completing a musical based on Hivnor's *Ticklish Acrobat*. ("Ned darling, you've got to make *money!* Put your fingers in *every* pie! Take Broadway by *storm!* You're more gifted than *anyone!* Herbert will make you *famous!"*) However, I doubt if this collaboration will leave ground: it's difficult to be simple. Especially for me—accustomed to writing recital songs, straightforward but for skilled voices with wide ranges—it's harder to tailor the tune than for, say, Auric, whose "serious" music is so knotty that when he sits down to compose a hit he throws long-hair ideas out the window and comes up with a masterpiece like *Moulin Rouge*. Besides, it's not talent that gets you to Broadway, but patience and push and kowtowing to those tacky vulgarians who pull the strings. Money's not my goal, my ambitions lie elsewhere. And so do John's, really.

▼▼▼

Mary's Bar on Eighth Street. It is already eleven summers ago that John Myers and Frank Etherton worked there, whining the tunes Paul Goodman and I composed for them: *Bawling Blues, Jail-Bait Blues, Near Closing Time*. Occasionally, for comic relief, Eugene Istomin would play *Ondine* on the tuneless piano and the drunks would actually stop talking. Eighth Street's changed a lot but we have not. We are all for sale. And let's be careful. Because we aren't much maybe, but we're all we've got.

▼▼▼

Like sieves we should retain only what is needed. A first impression or sweet recollection can be wrecked by reworking. In before-&-after ads, in Hollywood overhauling of starlets, it's always the first version that's more authentic. A ballet rehearsed on an empty stage, an unfinished poem, seem often more expressive than a final product, for in them we perceive the honest labor procedures which artists later hide. As soon as the painter's given what he wanted, his job, for his purpose, is over. Of course there's always the being nice to rich people, though finishing schools (do they still exist?) don't make finer folks. Do I mean all that?

▼▼▼

Tomorrow I will make a record of five of my songs with Patricia Neway. And after that I'll go to the ballet with Libby Holman, who's lately been trying to convert me to Zen—except that I've always "had" it; it's just that now it's been given a title. It is the poor man as creative artist. There are thousands more saints than great composers.

The demon of sobriety. Perhaps all sober people are really drunks who don't know it. It is not fright. It is boredom.

For the past year my sexuality has been shabby, to say the least, through an increasing inability (or un-desire) to concede on American terms. Suddenly I'd rather live alone and hate it than à deux or en masse and hate it, and France seems so far off. To think I used to introduce myself by enclosing half-naked pictures in letters to people I'd never seen! Christmas will soon be here.

▼▼▼

Menotti concocted a truly eerie get-together at Chanler Cowles'. "Everyone" was there, from Auden to Zadkine, but mostly younger genii gleaned by Steven Vinaver. The purpose was for Great Minds to commune and eventually collaborate, at the fee of one hundred dollars per contribution, on what would become an evening of Album Leaves next summer at Spoleto. The eeriness came from the silence, a silence not of communion but of embarrassment, since conversation between Great Minds is not easy and we know what its dearth leads to. So at the liquor tray near which I'm standing demurely in a pink bow tie given me by Bill Inge, Jack Kerouac approaches and, with a twick, undoes the tie, saying, "You're a doll." "So are you." "Yes, but I like girls." "Well, that's your problem." . . . Edward has already finished his *Sandbox*, Lukas Foss his *Hellos and Goodbyes* and me with Jay Harrison *Last Day*. [Not one of which was done at Spoleto.—N.R. 1967]

▼▼▼

Dîner en ville with Marc B. and Libby. Then the latter and I go to a church lecture by Alan Watts. Libby Holman is not only the world's one real female baritone capable of sustaining a consonant (and it cannot be done!), but the world's thinnest lady with a plump character: *joie de vivre* of Sarah Bernhardt. I think I love her.

▼▼▼

Last night late and glutted, stretching like a reptile and blasé as Nero, I rolled over and said to the twenty-year-old: "Now I crave something new: nightingales' tongues or twelve red flowers to swallow." This morning I received a dozen roses with an attached note to hope I was still hungry. There are, then, pleasures from pain (or is it the pain of pleasure?). The consolation is in knowing that half of New York is as devastatedly dehydrated as I from the Christmas holidays. But I have not written a note in three months—and that can leave me even higher and dryer.

▼▼▼

It's a nice day. I'm reading the Pasternak novel with passion. Dear Eva Gauthier has died. Tomorrow is New Year's Eve. I could wish to be elsewhere. Here I don't speak of the world's state, but I suppose my own echoes it almost blow by blow. China like an enchanted princess comes out of a thousand years' sleep.

▼▼▼

And why do I keep on writing this journal? Probably nobody else will ever read it, and when *I* do there is no chronology to keep interest nor have ideas been helpfully clarified. Fear of anonymity can be also a terrific time-waster; and finally, in the third convolution which brings us back wiser to the starting place, all that really counts is eating and sniffing and dreaming and hearing parrots scream and seeing stars and faces and feeling speechless love—but *knowing* and being *aware* of these things. *Not* diaries, for God's sake, and no lamentations! All I've spoken so longly on what the artist is (he only for whom there is no definition) has been merely a rational evasion of my own lack of dedication through too much concern with personal physical effects: my living's too divided between sociability and creation: hence alcohol as blinding joiner. Age, or rather, decrepitude, is boredom of body. I wrote before that our flesh is willing but the spirit grows weak, repeating ourselves nevertheless in spirit like the seasons which rejuvenate each year as we crumble, crumble. What we are, and what we think we need, can be mutually exclusive. Wanting love is not coping with love. I have nevertheless always had my cake and eaten it. Tonight to end the year I'll get drunk at Norman Singer's.

PART 10
New York, Saratoga, Buffalo
1959–60

> *As for me I would exhibit my qualities, but I am not hypocrite enough to conceal my vices.*
>
> —LAUTRÉAMONT

1959, New Year's Day
And I did. It's raining. Have an awful cold. Excess is my name. But maybe why I stay young is that I never *spend* any of myself. Does this mean I've never *bought* anything *with* myself? Beginning with the word "treble" I knew I was going to commit suicide, and was glad. As recently as six years ago I didn't know (or rather, consider) the difference between a soprano and a mezzo. Yet some of my best vocal works had already been composed. Suicide from boredom. Suicide of boredom. The suffering of boredom. Suffering of waiting. Of expectation . . . *Male* is the principle character of this story. His younger brother Joan grew up nice and normal. (Remember to reread Kafka's *Metamorphosis*.)

In spite of it all (the conditioning) I am American and eat just in order to smoke, drink to screw (the next day). But the next day (hungover) I do not smoke (though I do eat). Oh, I do feel older and not "with all my life before me." The separation of the generations is so apparent, and here am I at the turning point, on a cliff. And still having the power to *will* love, yet without power to undo the suicide of waiting. American, without power not to feel guilty not to have created in months, but to have drunk, to have waited, to have squandered. The joys of glory are slim but doubtless tougher than the joys of failure. The real glory is *during* the work—when it doesn't count. (America, America.) Pasternak has certainly a different will from mine. Americans have never taken time for The Tragic. I said we

181

wrote diaries to scold a public that doesn't react. Falling in love is
always wonderful, and being in love always a bit boring.

It is very cold, very sunny. I am about to write a ballet with
Valerie Bettis whose father just died.

▼▼▼

What is waste? Where is it real, i.e., unhelpful? Is drinking, is
masturbation, waste? Is death? When can we learn from it?
More and more (in flashes, but increasingly frequent) I am
concerned with dying. But don't let anyone stop me from crying:
my routine cannot change. What's the difference between angel
and ape? There's nothing like the regrets of a hangover to keep
you in love. Those self-imposed obstacles that make plants
bloom.

At least the well-ordered man has time for everything. If he
says he hasn't *time* to read it's just that he doesn't *like* to. He has
time to love and read and work. He has time even to waste time.
He's capable of all, and all these things run parallel but at
different speeds, like our two lives. Time's one thing we can
helpfully waste. It can be done, though not by Miss Average
Man.

▼▼▼

Beauty centers in the eyes. Narcissus is ugly since his eyes do
not look out but in, projecting nothing.

▼▼▼

> *There is no man who differs more
> from another than he does from him-
> self at another time.*
>
> —PASCAL

Saratoga Springs, June 1959

Here at Yaddo I am far from writing the nature of things I
would have written if I'd written here these last five months of

silence because I'm far from the things that obsessed me staying near them, namely too much of the city and its contents.

For the record it should be mentioned that last spring two of my symphonies were played in New York within a fortnight of each other. Lenny Bernstein conducted gorgeously the world premiere of the Third Symphony with his Philharmonic in April. It was the best performance of anything I've ever had anywhere: from that score of two million flytracks Lenny brought forth sounds I'd not known I'd placed there. Jay Harrison later wrote that the piece was all about being young and loving it; actually it was composed as a five-movement lament for Claude. The juxtaposition of interpretations is less ironic than the fact that the first rehearsal (which for a performance of such importance is a composer's most precious moment) coincided precisely with my appointment for an interview with Unemployment Insurance renewal. When I explained this incomprehensible situation to the interviewer (couldn't we hurry a little?) his answer was *Huh!* Of such is the stuff of our nation. So I left, met Shirley, and we rushed through the afternoon to Carnegie Hall where some two hundred of what I took to be Girl Scouts were assembled with special passes to attend the rehearsal. For their delectation Lenny, upon reaching the silent 2/4 measure on page 27, let loose a Cossack-type shriek which impelled the whole orchestra into their jazzy quadruple-fortissimo entrance. The Girl Scouts were thrilled, as was I, and though the yell was not repeated in performance, it shall of course be incorporated into the final publication. As to the content of the music, so much had altered my outer and inner selves since it was written that I hardly recognized it, much less recalled the conditions under which it was made. On the same program, though, was Bill Russo's new piece whose attractive last movement featured Maynard Fergusen's trumpet which, like Truman Capote's opinions, sometimes reached pitches only dogs can hear, sticking out like a sore thumb and rather sounding like one. . . . In early May the Second Symphony received its local premiere in Town

Hall under Arthur Lief. And, oh yes, last February Bill Flanagan and I (with Patricia Neway) inaugurated to Standing Room Only the first in what we hope will be a series called *Music for the Voice by Americans*. So my winter's not been completely sour and profitless. Especially since Buffalo University's invited me to be a professor there for a year, and I guess I've accepted despite the fact that they don't know that I don't know anything about music.

I believe when I leave that—being gone—nothing will change: but everything does. I believe when I leave that (being gone) all will change. Nothing does.

I think as a plant, want to *be* a plant, *am* a plant.

Gold cake filled with ants is your lover left for the whorehouse. But one of these ants is someone else's gold cake, nor can we all think similar to what we see.

It is no accident that density's an anagram of destiny and rhymes with intensity.

During these five months Frank Etherton, the trial of us all, finally committed suicide in Cuba.

Drunkenness (for me) offers a necessary contrast to the body the way apparently wars do to a massive soul.

This year (the "season" from October to May) has for me stood still. It's closed now—with The Dresden Amen. Have I chosen my own condition?

Art *is* a camp, let us face it (*let's* face it). So's suicide . . . (comment on elision).

The most feminine of the masculine is still infinitely more masculine than the most masculine of the feminine. (Or: queens in drag are still butcher than bulldikes.) Ah! the humorless camp, the campless humor of it all! "Oh, he's a real she-devil! She was a real man: much muscles, much hair! (much feathers!)." So Jake and Tony then removed the pins from their silver hair which fell to the shoulders. Little Mrs. Pearl Fisher just laughed to see such sport, and so did Miss Joyce Twelve. They filled out the application blanks as follows:

Sex: male   Sex: housewife
Occupation: housewife   Occupation: male
                         Sex: Italian
                         Sex: √

There are games for which I no longer have the patience, and no one ever does the unexpected anymore.

Now I want to say it, *Now!* And by the time it's printed it won't make any difference anymore. . . .

Not Venice, but memories of Venice.

▼▼▼

I don't like cripples (including especially the blind), or the aged, or children (their self-conscious vanity), or the Chinese, or the irritating and noisy confusion of women's purses, and elbows and voices.

And I don't like people who say Cleop*ah*tra (instead of Cleop*ay*tra), or H*igh*awatha (instead of H*ee*awatha), or seerup (instead of surup), or *cairamell* (instead of carmel).

But time passes and once again I can admire the greatness of Rachmaninoff, of Sibelius.

▼▼▼

NED ROREM
Will commit suicide
next Tuesday the 24th at 9:30 P.M.
in his New York apartment—247 West 13 Street
You are cordially invited to attend.

R.S.V.P.

▼▼▼

(He used to be as handsome as he is today.)

▼▼▼

Till now I've not conceded nor taken the world on any but my own terms. As for the Beat Generation—we learn only what we

wish to learn. How are these parties different from those I've
been attending all my life? Ginsberg lacks the dignity of Sartre
because he practices what he *thinks* he preaches! The followers,
almost by definition, can never really grasp their leaders'
thoughts; but they have more "fun." They preach what they
practice.

▼▼▼

Unfortunately I can't get it up for people with money. I'm as
ashamed of using the key of C as of biting my fingernails or
liking cake. For this is self-indulgence and the easiest way out. I
am vaguely hysterical and frightfully calm; I have kissed my
own lips. (No: my own lips have kissed me.)

I never mean what I say. If that statement is true, it is
therefore false. Ad infinitum. I never say what I mean, nor do
the French who converse on simultaneous levels and take any
side so long as the speech may glitter and rebound like a tennis
racket or (as in the case of Cocteau) a silver handball. But
Americans take things at face value, which makes them so
boring in the parlor and terrifying in bed. "Hope I'll be as pretty
as you when I'm your age," said the elderly gentleman to the
blind nymphet. Lana Turner backward becomes Anal Renrut.

▼▼▼

While watching carp in the lake of Yaddo:

If all life—or more generally, all creation—results from the
union of male with female, then couldn't our galaxy be such an
offspring, a birth bang? Couldn't the answer be found in searching with telescopes those parents, and theirs and theirs, and their
extending like a V forever? In the beginning were two words:
father and mother. . . . Do we inhabit a masculine or feminine
universe? Will it eventually divide like the amoeba or mate like
a man?

▼▼▼

Tomorrow I return to Manhattan where (since my apartment's sublet) Libby [Holman] will let me use her top floor and piano for a couple of weeks. And thank God! because I've got all these *speeches* to write about music from inside out. From there I'll go to Philly for a month, then to Maggy Magerstadt's in Fish Creek for another month, and then—O Lord—to Buffalo! Libby, meanwhile, has become a loyal and hospitable friend— just at a time when I was convinced I'd never allow more people into my life. Naturally, like anyone not born rich she's unclear about that money beyond cultivating the widest variety of daffodil in America and sponsoring her own recitals which are more stimulating than anyone's in this dead day of the voice. Eventually she'll turn away from the crippled, the lost, the vain, and get solidly married. Then I shall lose her, as one loses most of one's men friends and all of one's women friends with weddings.

▼▼▼

Order is the acceptance of incompatibility. Or: marriage is chaos accepted.

▼▼▼

> I've often thought that I would like
> To be the saddle of a bike.
>
> —AUDEN

Zeus and Hera quarreled, each claiming the other's sex was more capable of gratification. To prove the point they called in the hermaphrodite Teresias.

"Who has more fun in bed, Teresias, man or woman?"

"Woman."

In fury Hera struck Teresias blind. In compassion Zeus bestowed foresight upon him.

> For so hard I think on man the thought crumbles into absolute unnature. . . .
>
> —PAUL GOODMAN

The bachelor, simply because he's used to it, will confront oncoming solitude with more felicity and circumspection than the widower. Now the confirmed bachelor is probably pederastical, since the sexuality of 99 out of 100 unmarried men over forty is suspect, and the 100th is no Casanova but a hermit. Of course it doesn't follow that a homosexual is more circumspect and felicitous than a hetero (we know better), but then again it's not sure he's *less* so. But he *is* more versed in loneliness, thanks to his dubious talent for promiscuity.

> *I speak of it as a thing with a future*
> *as yet badly done by amateurs neglecting*
> *the opportunity to be discriminating.*
>   —KAY BOYLE

A turkish bath, like the Quaker service, is a place of silent meeting. The silence is shared solely by men, men who come uniquely together not to speak but to act. More even than the army, the bath is by definition a male, if not a masculine, domain. (Though in Paris, whimsically, it's a lady who presents you your *billet d'entrée*, robe and towel.) There are as many varieties of bath as of motel, from the scorpion-ridden hammams of Marrakech, where like Rimbaud in a boxcar you'll be systematically violated by a regiment, to the carpeted saunas of Frisco, where like a corpse in a glossy morgue you'll be a slab of flab on marble with Musak. There is no variety, however, in the purpose served: anonymous carnality. As in a whorehouse, you check interpersonal responsibility at the door; but unlike the whorehouse, here a *ménage* might accidentally meet in mutual infidelity. The ethical value too is like prostitution's: the consolation that no one can prove you are not more fulfilled by a stranger (precisely because there's no responsibility to deflect your fantasies—fantasies which now are real) than by the mate you dearly love, and the realization that Good Sex is not in performing as the other person wants but as you want. You will reconfirm this as you retreat into time through every bath of history.

For decades there has existed in central Manhattan one such establishment, notorious throughout the planet but never written about. Certainly this one seeks no publicity: word of mouth seems sufficient to promote its million-dollar business. Located in the heart of a wholesale floral district, there's small chance that an unsuspecting salesman might happen in for a simple rub-down, the nearest hotel being the Martha Washington—for women only. The customers do constitute as heterogeneous a cross section as you'll ever find. (There are only two uncate-gorizable phenomena: the care and feeding of so-called creative artists, and the nature of a Turkish bath's clientele.) Minors and majors, beatniks and bartenders, all ages and proclivities of the married and single, the famous and tough, so *many* from Jersey! but curiously few mad queens because it's hard to maintain a style stark naked. To run across your friends is less embarrassing than cumbersome: who wants gossip now?

You enter at any age, in any condition, any time of night or week, pay dearly for a fetid cubicle, and are given a torn gown and a pair of mismated slippers (insufficient against the grime that remains in your toes for days). You penetrate an obscure world, disrobe in private while reading graffiti, emerge rerobed into the public of gray wanderers so often compared to the lost souls of Dante, although this geography is not built of seven circles but of four square stories each capable of housing some eighty mortals. Once, you are told, this was a synagogue; today it's a brothel lit like *Guernica* by one nude bulb. The top floor is a suite of squalid rooms giving onto a corridor from *The Blood of a Poet* with background music of a constant pitty-pat, whips and whispers, slurps and groans. The second floor, more of same, plus massive dormitory. On the ground floor are cubicles, a television room, a monastic refectory. The basement contains fringe benefits: a dryer, a massage room, a large dirty pool, and the famous steam-room wherein *partouzes* are not discouraged.

The personnel, working in shifts, comprises at any given time some ten people, including two masseurs and a uniformed policeman. Each of these appears dull-witted due to years of inhaling the gloomy disinfectant of locker room and hamburger grease.

There are feast and fast days, rough Spanish mornings and sneaky afternoons, even Embryo Night at the Baths. Eternal motion, never action (meaning production): despite a daily ocean of orgasm the ceaseless efforts at cross-breeding could hardly make a mule. Not from want of trying: at any time you may witness couplings of white with black, beauty with horror, aardvark with dinosaur, panda with pachyderm, skinny-old-slate-gray-potbelly-bald with chubby-old-slate-gray-potbelly-bald, heartbreakingly gentle with stimulatingly rugged—but always, paradoxically, like with like. Your pupils widen as a faun mounts that stevedore, or when a mountain descends on Mohammed. Some cluster forever together in a throbbing Medusa's head; others disentangle themselves to squat in foggy corners, immobile as carnivorous orchids, waiting to "go up" on whatever passes. There's one! on his knees, praying with tongue more active than a windmill in a hurricane, neck thrown back like Mata Hari's and smeared with tears nobody notices mingling with steam. All are centered on the spasm that in a fraction switches from sublime to ridiculous, the sickening spasm sought by poets and peasants, and which, like great love, makes the great seem silly. . . . Yet if at those suburban wife-swapping gang-bangs there's risk of pregnancy, these mirthless matings stay sterile—not because the sexes aren't mixed but because the species *are*.

If you don't believe me, says Maldoror, go see for yourself. You won't believe it *of* yourself, the money and months you've passed, a cultured person lurking in shadows governed by groin! Did you *honestly* spend the night? Can you, with your splitting head, manage it down the hall to pee, through shafts of black sunlight and idiot eyes and churning mouths that never say die, and crunched on the floor those tropical roaches you hadn't noticed last evening? Don't slip in the sperm while retching at the fact that it's 8 A.M. and there's still a dull moan and a sound of belts (they've really no sense of proportion). So leave, descend while cackling still rends the ear, reclaim that responsibility checked with your wallet. Hate all those bad people; or, if you will, feel lightened and purged. Allow the sounds to dim—the anticlimatic puffing and shooting and slippery striving, the friendless hasty jerkings that could fertilize a universe in the dirty dark (*quel embarras de richesses!*). Quit the baths to go home and bathe, but make clear to yourself that such uncommitted hilarity doesn't necessarily preclude a throbbing heart. For three times there you found eternal love.

▼▼▼

With "Oedipal types" it's not mothers but fathers that are loved and sought.

▼▼▼

Buffalo, November 1959
    Again, five months later.
    I write less and less in this book. Instead of daily, weekly, it's now semi-annually, and even then without length or drive. Journals, of course, are a European preoccupation; and here in America, after more than two years, my interests are centered elsewhere than autobiography (though certainly—alas! perhaps—not in love affairs). So there is not an urge to explain how I've come to Buffalo as professor in the 37th year, but only to notate the accumulated store of anecdotes, now devoid of spontaneity.

▼▼▼

Why must every day be an exceptional day for me? killing myself in order to live? The pretense of caring. Literally. Not a week passes but I consider suicide—the vanity of bars, of people, of liquor, of work. Locked in the cage of veins, the constricting net that still (at thirty-six) Christianly inhibits adventure. Then abandon myself to it (only, though, with wine), finding always what I most abhor yet most perceive: mediocrity. Thoughts gain order today in talking of music (not writing it), and scant need of diaries.

How recite the death toll so long later? Billie Holiday went in July with more tears from me than for Landowska in August. She reigned undiminishing and ever-glamorous over my generation.

Excessive moderation. My dying words will be: "When I grow up—!"

▼▼▼

I am now a professor at Buffalo University. This diary will therefore by definition become "A Self-Portrait of an Artist as a Middle-Aged Man." But *Self-Portrait* implies a certain objective knowledge I no longer have: today I understand less about me than ever: I may know what I am, but not who. *Artist* once implied a man of superior, or at least special, qualities set apart either by himself or by society; in that sense the word is now completely out of fashion. And *middle-aged* suggests precisely that, and is a state which, though I may be facing it, I don't wish to focus on.

As for Art with a capital *A*, it no longer means anything—at least to the young who now make the laws, set the tone, dictate the future. For them art is where they find it, not necessarily framed in museums or formally presented from concert stages by genteel conductors or ladies in long dresses. It is no longer in the sacrosanct creation of one ego who signs his name big, but rather in the thawing snow out there, or happening among us here (*happening* is specifically the word), in the environment, the popular, the communal. For the first time ever there is a new definition, the only restrictions being time and space—and then not always. The nineteenth-century of worshipful romantic ostracism is over, and we have retreated—or rather advanced again—into a period of group communication, although the subject matter is usually "lack of communication," at least in the movies, which are today's healthiest expression.

Today's *un*healthiest expression is music, which, inasmuch as it has serious intentions, has become, for elite and commoner alike, a great big bore. Throughout the planet there has been disseminated a disgust for sound. Accomplished musicians and sophisticated laymen alike no longer find listening to concert music very attractive. This is partly due to the oversaturation of music through Muzak (you can look away from paintings, but you can't listen away from pieces), partly to the standardization of subscription concerts which play only Beethoven, and partly (so far as the avant-garde is concerned) to the intellectualization of music which paradoxically alienates the intellectuals. The "In" audiences today (as usual, a Mutual Admiration Society) may cheer loud, but the cheering is mirthless. As to ecstatic swooning, perish the thought! The language, having become academically accepted internationally, is now a sort of neutralized Esperanto devoid of character; everyone's writing the same piece somewhat as Action Painters all paint one picture. It's not facetiously that I esteem jazz (or folk, or rock, or whatever it's called) more highly than I do most of my so-called serious colleagues. These new young performers at their best make tunes equal to Schubert—better, so far as I'm concerned— harmonies more satisfying than the most ingenious Frenchman, and perform with the nuance of our greatest vocalists against orchestrations that have at once more ingenuity and simplicity than anyone else's. Their real power for the young though of course comes through their words, their poems.

For it's the vocal or visual, not the abstract-auditory, which are the preemptive arts today: they echo most coherently the incoherence of our time. Which is why movies are now the healthiest expression. (Though for me they always were.) Young artists, what's more, seem less and less involved with easel painting, and more and more with the movable. They turn to movies or to choreography.

Whereas for over a decade American music—*all* music—has been treading water in the four currents of serial, jazz, chance, and (for want of a better term) conservative, which flowed from different directions toward an ultimate point without merging or broadening or bursting into a geyser. The composers, floundering in an *embarras de richesses* and unsure about which way to turn, ended by turning away from music and toward prose. Their prose was an explication of their work, since it was no longer possible, as the saying goes, to let the music speak for itself. Whatever the future holds by way of purely musical vitality, the American composer as a verbally articulate phenomenon (contrary to the painter or movie-maker who practice trades which, for the moment, are more vigorous than music and so don't need explaining) has come to be the accepted thing today.

The art of music (or the craft of sound, or whatever you now choose to call it) is. . . .

▼▼▼

My discipline avoids the actual. Whenever I pick up a newspaper my mind wanders. On purpose?

I count things, everything, why? Count and recount the pendants on Ellen Adler's chandelier, recount and recount the spots on Bill Flanagan's wall, the strands in his rug; count and count again the notes on a staff in my brain. A mania, phobia of counting. Why? Could it be I'm a 12-toner *manqué?*

▼▼▼

The young today, it seems, all smoke pot. How *démodé* my drinking seems to them. And yet to me how *démodé* already is their psychoanalysis which gears them to accept rather than to examine bourgeois standards.

▼▼▼

Anecdotes are a diary's heart's blood. Yet their annotation requires more skill and patience than philosophic musings (not to mention love affairs, which are immobile). Comedy, as everyone knows, is tougher than tragedy.

▼▼▼

I make lists. To remind myself of everything, even to shit. The lists are iron rules—what was written must be performed. To remind myself even to make a list. Existence is a list. This book, in a sense, is a mere reminder that I have lived. . . . Oh words, words, why? Is there not intelligent silence? Does anyone care, finally, that the musician has *expressed* himself? Could he not sit merely on a park bench considering how he doesn't wish to notate, to notate forever, but let his posterity be absorbed and—so to speak—disseminated by the fabulous clouds?

And if this book, these books, are ever published in hard print, how much will be even myself of the past?

▼▼▼

What if I now were to say (to confess!) that this whole diary's been a hoax, a red herring, a fiction to make myself interesting! Would (could) it, for that, *be* a hoax? Are my lies lies, and therefore the truth? Could even I know the answer? Do I? You'll never know!

▼▼▼

I've never let myself go all the way—in loving, suffering, drinking, composing. Each is reined to prevent its infringing on the others. So they all diminish.

To feel, one must think. Yet to think—at least for me—precludes feeling. Seldom have I loved for the "sake" of loving, to have loved and lost, that is, been lost in love—in the *act* of love. Though surely I've been lost in the *thought* of love. I think I feel.

▼▼▼

An artist's duty is not to present solutions, but to clarify dilemmas so that the public will seek solutions. For an artist is concerned with ALL, and "all" has no one solution. If a man is capable of resolving satisfactorily his exposed dilemma, the dilemma is by definition limited; so such a man is not an artist but a scientist or craftsman. I'm not sure I believe this—at least insofar as it relates to music.

▼▼▼

Another gorgeous torture: lack of privacy. To be forever naked and alone within an illuminated plate-glass cell surrounded by an audience rotating twenty-four hours a day. But (not unironically) you are permitted any behavior.

▼▼▼

Must there be a point to every story? Do you like killing two birds with one stone? . . . Rich Chinese, it's told, once feasted on the raw gray matter of living monkeys. After fixing the animal's head in a vise, the gourmet took a jade instrument which, in one whack, scalped the creature like a soft-boiled egg, exposing alive the delicacy of its steaming brains. Like the eggs and meat provided by today's factory-poultry which are, so to speak, born in their coffins, the skull of a monkey (as he expired) once provided both soup dish and soup.

—*Et pourtant vous serez semblable à cette ordure . . .*

▼▼▼

The girl with the bat in her hair screams so loudly she can't hear the screams of the bat.

▼▼▼

Inconvenience of coincidence. Two lovers (desperately, intimately in love), on saying good-bye in the morning make a date for that evening. But during the day they unexpectedly meet on the street. What can they say to each other now? What, out in the busy world where both are pressed for time?

▼▼▼

After a labyrinthine correspondence with Theodore Roethke, letters of practical suspicion and mutual praise, the settings of his eight poems are finally completed for Alice Esty. Because— and not despite the fact that—my heart wasn't in them, they've turned out to be great songs. (For musicians the heart is a dangerous vulgarian.) To celebrate, I took a long weekend away from the strenuous Buffalo blizzards and flew to New York for the usual pastimes.

Edward [Albee] took me to his *Zoo Story* which plays even better than it reads, and which he himself observed as for the first time with that damn inscrutable Cheshire smile. He's clearly quite pleased with himself, as I too am with him; and now, never really having had him, I shall lose him forever since, in a manner of speaking, he too's had a wedding.

Jay Harrison, housed with not only Jane and their two infant daughters but now with his stepmother, the maid, the nurse, and a female English sheepdog named Oboe, declares in distraction: "Do you realize I'm living surrounded by twenty-two tits!" (The dog has five pair.)

▼▼▼

Nice ladies sit with their legs together, virile gents with theirs apart, contrary to the positions they'll probably assume in sexual intercourse.

And now I'm back in the snows of the north.

▼▼▼

A student contralto asks: "Before I sing this song of yours, Mr. Rorem, could you explain what the words mean?" "The words mean what my music tells you they mean." What more do I know about poetry?

▼▼▼

On the bus I sit next to a girl engrossed in *The Buffalo Evening News*. Her bovine eyes are caressing an image of myself printed there in advertisement of next week's concert. I lean over to see more clearly. She turns on me with a snarl.

▼▼▼

Well, yes I did go back to Chicago for three days last August—to hear Wallenstein do my symphony at Ravinia—and then on to visit dear Maggy in Wisconsin. The return, and mescaline, were the *important* events of my thirties. How not to cry when nothing changes but one's self? When for the first time in thirteen years one visits the scene of childhood crimes? Nothing, *nothing* was different, except there were no parents to call out to. Sunlit vines on our building were no thicker than memory; smells, wind, the time of day, converged to make the past the present. The recall of roller skates, easy on the tarred street, less pleasant on the rough cement, that cement which still contained a clean N.R. scrawled there a quarter-century back when it was soft. The bright Chekhovian parlor where first I wrote music, and thought of (and practiced) the sexual privileges (stigmas at least have benefits). Bruce Phemister rescued me from brooding as we covered all Hyde Park at sunset, past the Oriental Institute and "Juliet's Garden" of the Theological Seminary, past Jackman Field, where our high school ghosts playing goalies gave a lackadaisical kick at the soccer ball—preferring to discuss Debussy or Dietrich, past his mother's lilac garden which so many thousand midnights ago intoxicated our poems. Lake Michigan, and her saxophones of the Palm Grove Inn wailing into the summer watered lights purpler than the cake frosting we swam in. Was it us? Or was that all I can really write now for another five months?

PART 11

Saratoga, New York, Buffalo, New York

1960–61

"How wonderful to be alive," he
thought.
*"But why does it always hurt? God
exists, of course. But if He exists, then
it's me."*
—FROM *Doctor Zhivago*

Mais, vrai, j'ai trop pleuré.
—RIMBAUD

Yaddo (Saratoga Springs) June 1960

Not five, but more than seven. And only a few pages back I was in Yaddo a year ago.

The odor of orange on my fingertips retrieved Morocco today in a flashing dream of the whole decade, doubtless because I'm engaged in reading (with a certain enjoyable boredom) the Durrell tetralogy.

The diary, recording, somehow removes the bloom from memory. The scrapbook is a morgue. But anonymity still scares; and if now I see that old photographs prevent new life, I know too I'll really die. Which is why I don't tell tales here (or even *write* any longer)—but eat, like a child and monkey, my own pubic lice, crabs, *quoi de plus naturel?* The world (my own) of that stranger, the heart of the crotch—complete and complacent— goes off and ignores me into other worlds. We go nowhere. So I write in the air (have you tried it?). Write in the air and attempt to separate the words. You can't. The invisible ink retreats oozing into the clenched fist more maddening than the weary slapstick of vaudevillians with scotch tape.

Sailor. Sailors. Feeling almost assured the café was empty, I nevertheless had to see for myself. It was. But no sooner home than I felt it filling up. On returning, to my horror, I found it overrun.

▼▼▼

Women argue that they've never been given a chance. Chances are taken, not given.

▼▼▼

Poets, why do they complete their public readings: "And now, to end on a cheerful note"! Would they say this if their chief preoccupation were *not* cheerful? To leave behind the truest ectoplasm they'd do better to end on a somber note.

A painter with his variety of styles through the years retains a same signature. No, not even his handwriting alters.

Inscription, latrine wall, men's room of Deco's, Washington Street, Buffalo: "Tom I was here again please come back."

Glad you're glad I'm glad you're . . . Do not compare yourself to me though both admire the smell of man. Yet I am disinterested in anyone who is disinterested in me. I'm ever more disinterested!

▼▼▼

Bobby Cone's drowning: most shocking is that the intellectual cannot die a shepherd's death. (Exposure.) Yet he did. At best the intellectual dies of suicide, old age, or heart attacks; at worst in auto wrecks or of drink. But as victim to the elements? Words speak louder than actions.

"*Si j'étais un homme,*" she said to me, "*j'aimerais te baiser.*" . . . The panic of cities. In Buffalo starlings annoyed me at 5 A.M. There, even *after* the auto wreck, I remained drunk.

▼▼▼

Death toll (at the new year): Camus, Margaret Sullivan, Ankey Larrabee.

Some people still do care. (I *think!*) Awfully.

▼▼▼

I've met and experienced everyone and thing I've desired. Now to compose that which I must. Or rather to come to life. Come to Death? END is an anagram of NED. Oh.

▼▼▼

July (Yaddo)
Boredom springs eternal in the human breast. Not to speak of the suffocating shock of sterility now that I'm *supposed* to create. Yaddo's a luxurious concentration camp where I can neither camp nor concentrate, hence the luxury's guilt-making. While everyone else is busy doing poems and pieces and pictures (as though it made a difference) I stay reading, wondering why I have to be a composer—still, still dictated by terms of alcohol and unoriginal sin. Their outside impression is of my gross generalities, when really I'm (not so much aggressively shy as) bored, bored, the mind miles off. But off where?

▼▼▼

Fourteen years ago Klaus Mann stung my thigh with morphine and killed himself. Yes, the diary, the scrapbook stunts, sucks, and gluts, allows experience only for the sake of altered memories. So I fly with voluptuous gluttony out into a night of the park to see about living. Grand illusion of love, of even sex. Flinging mucous or fingernails about, or sperm, or hairs in a comb, sections of Ned scattered in earth. An impotent three weeks—and in three months or more I'm thirty-seven.

But there are tantalizing contemplative consolations. For instance the dolphins. We now learn of their intelligence, their undersea language. They've glided far past logic not caring that they don't know that they know that they just like happily *to be.* Aren't we finally wise enough for migration into water? We'll walk upside-down on the undersurface of the lake (mirroring Jesus) as though gravity were in the sky. Swim *down* to the surface. Conspire with the porpoise. Smart purpose.

Well, at least Nature (as they say) is all around, notably in the form of baby swallows (I could use a grown-up swallow), daily hurricanes, and (when I walk into Saratoga for the laundry or something) massive mosquito flocks holding on like pilot fish. Do I indeed stand in my own way, fashion my own impediments? Or suffer, like others here, from a terrible handicap (!): no talent. It's not talent but enthusiastic patience, a missing ingredient. I'd rather go deaf than blind. But I'm not *visual! Mais justement!* In Europe, not being a "success" doesn't mean you're a flop.

I said to Joe LeSueur: "I've decided to become charitable." His answer: "Really? How do you intend to go about it?" And he quotes Maugham: "It's not enough that I succeed, my friends must fail." Then adds: "It's not enough that I fail, my friends must fail."

The difference between that eternal aggravation: "What do you like?" "Everything," and: "What do you like?" "Anything."

Communication. How I hate the word. Communication indeed!

Tonight we saw northern lights. Green.

Am I also really going to die? *La vie s'arrête pile.* The breath is caught. Can't believe it.

▼ ▼ ▼

My Flute Trio is finished and never have I written a work with less enthusiasm. The drunken spontaneity is, for me, today gone from *all* music. On the other hand I'm obsessed with my theater. Yet, seated before the famous blank sheet, about to type the first phrases of a drama, I write: Who am I to think of making a play? And even those words look pretentious. What? Humility! But it's not for nothing I've been fifteen years diaryzing. . . . Working title: *The Pastry Shop* (a monologue for Judith Malina).

Haven't had a drink in about eight weeks. Beginning to feel the need. I *must* sometimes, to allow the other "me" (more schizoid than Joanne Woodward's Eve) to get some air. And I *must* recall the hangover, the lovely hangover with a head like a sizzling watermelon when I sit on the toilet, scarcely human, reading praiseworthy clippings about myself, and thinking thickly: is that me? By accident two weeks ago I was offered a glass of tonic containing a *soupçon* of gin; my reaction disturbed for days; all or nothing is how it is since I was released from high school twenty summers back. Salt, salt in tangerine tones.

▼▼▼

"Sometimes it rains on Thursday," he lied. He always lied. And the dike who announced: "Be back later, kids. Gotta go home and take a shit, a shave and a shower."

For myself I have, in principle, stopped swearing.

Because of always falling in love with puzzling women I've solved the riddle through simple men. What a solution! Great emotions I put off till next week: ". . . he shrank from every connection with the actual because he saw therein a threat to the possible. The potential was his kingdom . . ."—*Dr. Faustus*

Povla Frijsh died last month. So did Ellie Kassman. "Death is the mother of beauty," said Wallace Stevens. Idyll, Idle, Idol, Ideal.

▼▼▼

August. In Philadelphia to visit Rosemary and her five children as antidote to a frenzied New York week of lust, liquor and laziness which in turn was antidote to two months of Yaddo where I painfully ejected a flute trio and easily produced a little play: *The Pastry Shop*. Yaddo is for me (have I said it?) *the concentration camp de luxe*—but purposed: starting today and tomorrow the days and tomorrows start to blend indistinguishably! But in New York days blend with *nights*—and each separate pair is jagged—not smooth; where all I do is drink, walk the streets, and when people say aren't you a composer? how can I stay home when other people don't—or if they do, how do they dare when I don't? Tonight I went with Rosemary to see Brigitte Bardot.

▼▼▼

Back in New York now. And more drinking, more and more, interlaced with movies and the turkish bath, hay fever and procrastination, dental devastating work and huge bills. Heat wave, and the day's a smear.

▼▼▼

Write children's piano pieces with as titles Colors & Days, Numbers & Months: Blue, Tuesday, Four, October, Yellow, Saturday, Seven, February. Some for right-hand alone, some for left.

Write a nonvocal piece on words, like Beethoven's *Muß es sein? Es muß sein!* Then eliminate the words. Or—going farther than Berio—set a poem, then sing it backwards, first by words, then syllables, finally letters. Symmetry. Or: song for two voices with overlapping of syllables: one voice continues where the other leaves off, in midstream. Also simultaneous crescendo and decrescendo on same note. . . . The word *gold* has six sounds, a double tripthong: guh-ah-oh-oo-ll-d.

Write a piece containing as much as possible of the hate I have for the world, for you, all you, of how alone I feel, how alone, yet how the aloneness will not be reduced by being less hateful.

September, chez Morris, Water Island
No I'm not particularly happy, yes I am particularly sad, and for reasons more concrete than fifteen years ago, namely, I'm fifteen years older, and do they stop dead in the street anymore? Of course no love. Depressed for this country we inhabit, which belongs to me as well as you, which we've destined for chaos soon. Thrill at visions of the young (who'd have thought it would come to that?), and Youth is Beauty, Beauty Youth.

Requiem for the West. Our work, if we like it, is the *compensation* which remains the most faithful friend. Such vivid bromides are in keeping with the lonesome fawn décor of this isle. "Well," they ask, "what is more terrible than unhappiness?" Oh, I don't know. Boredom, I suppose. Because unhappiness is at least active, whereas boredom has never, I think, made adrenalin flow. And time won't tell. Yet as Bill F. pointed out the other day: for the likes of *us* the future lies in a latrine.

October

Back in Buffalo. Cool already. Smell of bonfires and pencil shavings: going-back-to-school weather. Tom Prentiss in South Wales is a boon.

The Pastry Shop. Suddenly everyone's shocked at what I've written there. As though for twenty years I hadn't been composing obscenities in music! But what *is* obscene in the elusive "meanings" of nonvocal music? Light as black, heavy as white. Compose a hateful quarrel, all done softly.

▼▼▼

The other night without explanation I waited at home. The more I waited the more love grew. Three hours late the person arrived: love wilted on the spot.

An equality permitting dislike of certain Negroes as much as certain whites, a freedom to choose enemies as we choose friends. And that, without the scrutiny of "progressives" with inverted prejudice (everyone, provided he is an underdog, is good!) or the I-told-you-so attitude of "reactionaries" with more direct resentment (everyone, provided he is an underdog, is bad).

No white American can—under any circumstances nor by whatever transference—know what it is to be a Negro, because he does not of necessity think of himself as white, whereas the Negro of necessity always thinks of himself as black.

▼▼▼

Well, in those Manhattan weeks, the dentist revamped my bite to the tune of nearly $900. And I gave two parties. After the second one, while drinking a sixteenth gin-and-tonic at a bar *mal-famé* near the Cherry Lane Theater (the last of the disreputable taverns to tolerate my presence: in the Village now I'm permitted only in respectable bars!) a nondescript person engaged me in an *entretien* the upshot of which was that his envy of my person provoked a desire not for rape but for strangulation. I, being drunk, was intrigued, but understood (why explain) that he meant this, and that he had committed such "crimes" in the past. But when my friends approached he vanished, and I only recalled his words and nervous hands in my hungover sheets next day. Now I ask you, is this the proper company for America's tenth most-played composer?

▼ ▼ ▼

Yesterday I was thirty-seven. Ah. Today already it's snowing. That's Buffalo. Title: *The Disgusting Birthday*.

I am staying home from school (as when a child) with aches and sore throat, canceling appointments and just let the wind howl outside. Small wonder: overdrinking and overworking both with mediocre people. Drinking to get laid (and don't) and working on my speech and Weill's *Jasager* with a conscientiousness unfocused. Nobody knows what most people are talking about most of the time, but most of the time it makes no difference. A difference that's important is the (subtle) one between articulation and communication.

Yes, feeling sick, staying home, day and night drenched in soggy odiferous naps—you know. Not sick enough to sleep—too sick to work—just think and resent. About the shock of the famous. The shocks of growing up to see that great poets are not only personally as petty and vicious as "real people," but can also be fascist nigger-hating, fairy-baiters. What's more they fucked and despised me—those Chicago intellectuals of my childhood.

Am I fair?—being fair? Of course not: artists aren't fair. They just build better mousetraps. To tell them don't complain is more irrational than saying don't squeeze that pimple white-ripe and plangent.

Religion is through. Religion is really through. I realized this most clearly the other morning on awakening (too soon) from a hangover when all is not confused but—on the contrary—electrically delineated. Religion as such is a farce in America and no one can fail to feel this on some level.

Oh I'm ill and reeling. Today Mitropoulos died. Eilliott Carter's 2nd Quartet: four madmen yell in a language I can't understand but I know their words are wonderful. Or do I understand without knowing the tongue—like birds heard through mescaline, or angels through dreams? The world ends here: that's our art speech—and not *sans humour*.

Am not now interested in writing more music. That's no way for venting current spleen. Why don't they give me time to start and finish "The Voyeuse With Poor Vision"?

▼ ▼ ▼

Theater means: the artificial concentration of an event. All art is theater. The most tangible versions are staged.

In musical theater the broadest event is Opera, wherein a singer for several hours becomes someone else. The narrowest event is Song, wherein a singer for a brief moment becomes someone else. As to which projection is more difficult depends on training, and the emphasis of training depends on location in history.

Today we all seem more equipped for the Great Lie—the huge single schizoid split of opera, than for the White Lie, the small multiple-personality segments of the song recital. For singers this equipment is an economic necessity: there is simply no living except in opera. The young ones now are vocally oriented to decibels, psychologically to long-range transference. If ever they do sing songs they approach those songs as the obsolete is always approached—without a point of view—and usually mistreat them as arias, meaning as events bigger than life. A song is an intimate experience having less to do with mammoth scope than with miniature intensity. This last quality has become, at least in America, like a needle in a haystack. The needle is still occasionally sought and found by a rare few, such as Phyllis Curtin, who rub off the rust and try to make it serve again.

Phyllis last week braved northern New York's worst blizzard since 1902 and a fee one-fourth the size of her usual one, to fly here and prepare a Rorem-Poulenc recital (some twenty odd songs she'd never sung) simply from fondness for a dying medium and friendship for me. I love her. I love her voice even more. But I love mostly her way with a song, a way that makes her constantly a new person with each song sung, rather than the same person with each new song.

▼▼▼

And last Thursday. My squalid evening with the young J. It is not so much his shock as my own which disturbs. For how long is it now (fifteen years? twenty?) that I've been pulling the same fiasco, demolishing expressly my possibilities, destroying my angel by showing the whining devil—in short, killing the "thing I love"? And Friday I awoke to write this sort of hungover reflection: It hurts to look at you, you force abjection, abjection thank God, I can still be it, it: drunk—the only *proof* is suicide. Proof to whom?

Well. Beauty *does* hurt. Since then I've been torturing myself with hope. Wrong numbers sound. Phenobarbital doesn't work on me. For while it numbs my sick body, my sick brain burns and won't be undone.

(And Friday I found I'd written also this: Cloisters and sequences are my haven. Hot marble thoughts. Pink wasn't warm. Warm wasn't pink. Hot marble asses. Sequences and cloisters—my haven.)

And Esther Berger now has died. So told me Sylvia Marlowe whose fatal harpsichord case is coffin for a cyclops.

▼▼▼

January 1961

Over the holidays in Pittsburgh there was a forum on my music (very successful, of course) although Ormandy because of illness had to cancel *Eagles*. Parties for me in Pennsylvania: it's quite respectable to take the parents because they live there, while in Buffalo where I'm professor "composers don't have fathers"—though in a pinch I can take Mother.

This volume of the diary covers a larger span (already three and a half years) than the others—lately because of the plays and lectures and essays and teaching, plus now scant interest in love and name-dropping and recipes and blood.

Nevertheless I passed twenty Christmas days in Manhattan slush where for the new year I took Joe LeSueur to Ruth Ford's and there was Garbo. (Annually the Scotts receive what are called "celebrities," all very on-stage. When Garbo, uninvited, walked in, they were all suddenly off-stage. For who can do better? Joe whispered, "Is that who I *think* it is? Promise, that whether or not we meet her, we must say we did! Her eyes *are* larger than anyone's have a right to be.") Later Joe took *me* to 42nd Street where—I mean it!—I'd never been, and two days before I brought home at 5 A.M. a maniac who tore open my hand with a broken candlestick and I was stitched at Saint Vincent's, then next evening played good piano at Phyllis Curtin's. See, see, even such recent looking back makes you turn salty.

▼▼▼

I am not interested when a student explains: "But I *felt* it that way." Justification through emotion is worthless, in music as in law. Of *course* a composer has feelings or he wouldn't be composing. But those feelings can take care of themselves and will always show through. So I am interested in how they can be controlled. Now a verbal explication of such control is not so easy for the "inspired" type of composer who uses sheer sound as his guide, as for the "objective" type whose intellectual procedures are themselves the music. This second type is as exasperating as the first in that he categorically denies feelings as impetus. As a teacher, then, I get it both ways!

⏶ ⏶ ⏷

Taste, touch and smell are for sex (i.e., survival) while the eyes, the ears, are reserved for art.

Defiantly looking as *louche* as possible—because really we're waiting for Mother. Defiantly looking as innocent as possible—because really we're cruising.

▼ ▼ ▼

A writer needn't go out and live, but stay home and invent, crying himself to sleep occasionally.

"Do you know the *Missa Solemnis?*"
"No, who is she?"

Beethoven to his wife: "But you can't leave me! You're my inspiration!"
"Me your inspiration? That's a laugh!

Ha ha ha ha!"

▼ ▼ ▼

Who am I to be deferred to by students? I've only myself begun to be a composer.

▼ ▼ ▼

This evening, to the accompaniment of Fizdale & Gold, I made my debut as actor by reciting the Pierre Loüys texts to

Debussy's *Cinq Epigraphes Antiques* on my final lecture-recital
in Buffalo. During the question-and-answer period, when asked
my opinion of the symphony here, I replied that though it was
excellent it did not—like most American orchestras do not—perform enough new music. At which point Josef Krips (who has
beautifully played three works of mine, who had been my host
earlier in the evening, and who was now in the audience) got up
and walked out. This misunderstanding will eventually be resolved, for both Mitzi and Josef have been my good friends, and
real friends just don't nurse quarrels. But it's sad that we will
have to make up by mail, because tomorrow I leave permanently
for New York. . . . Meanwhile I only hope the students will
have gained half as much from me as I have from them: the best
thing about teaching is that you learn so much.

▼ ▼ ▼

Ides of March in the evening. The Buffalo stint is over. Back
in New York.

If I never write here anymore it's because I write nothing
nowhere. Haven't put down a note of music in six months—the
longest ever. Been six weeks back from Buffalo, a city that never
existed, harboring some unknown Ned Rorem who for a year
and a half did his job in a trance brilliantly, then vanished. As
indeed I have. Waiting, waiting immobile again for something
(what?) while others scurry ambitiously to money and love. It's
ambition here that breaks the spirit, sterilizing all endeavor: can
no longer work for pleasure. These New York weeks have been
blurred in frantic socializing, indiscriminate fucking, even more
indiscriminate drinking. An old story. Who am I trying to fool?
In less than three years I'll be forty. And next month I finally
return to France seeking the insane, the grey-haired, the dead
and dying, those caught in their own problems, and my not-
forgotten yet vanished boyhood. Still, this is no mistake. (I wrote
Virgil in Paris: "Have you seen my lost youth around?" He
answered: "There's plenty of lost youth around but I don't know

if any of it's yours.") It's not Paris but myself in Paris that I miss: those infinitesimal hotel rooms near Cluny with hot Algerians eleven years ago smelling of urine, novelty, despair, and *gros rouge* with radishes at noon.

▼▼▼

Like torture, only worse. To parody Poe: Manhattan's sadomasochistic alcoholism is "*S. and M. found in a Bottle.*" All nature is immune to human fleas. Witness: *People in the Snow.* Their awful, their ridiculous vulnerability. Drunk, G.L. spent the night—left his watch. A week later, drunk, some *inconnu* spent the night, stole the watch—which watch had not left its place on my mantel. I'm impervious to the inanimate ("possessions"), but that whole week a blizzard was moving, moving, killing us who are corpses on leave of absence.

▼▼▼

April Fool's Night. In three weeks I leave for Europe.

Lovers fade from these pages like Anna from *L'Avventura.* And how I like those new movies of Antonioni seen lately with frightening Ruth Yorck! They and she know how to put one in one's place. How much more agreeably troubling to watch the rich suffer than the poor (as with De Sica): their boredom and stupidity is the same, but they are *bored in ermine.* Anyway, why are the poor, by virtue of being poor, more virtuous and intelligent than the rich? As father likes to say: "Born of poor but dishonest parents."

Opera scene: twelve minutes of music *without* singing. She waits. She wonders—as in *L'Avventura.* But she never opens her mouth. Obviously a movie opera and for Antonioni, the only great man around these days, beyond definition, like a great beached whale.

Antonioni's star is the scenery. That's not just an aphorism: what we grow closest to and come to love is not the mobile name but the inanimate place which, framed by his camera, takes on a life of its own.

▼▼▼

The child says: when I grow up the important part will begin. As a grown-up he says: those first lost years were the important part.

▼▼▼

When will I learn about getting older? Well, look in the mirror! Yes, but it only lies concerning right and left (meaning right and wrong). The Late Late Show informs us better of our lives' lengths: those landmarks of yesternight, that close focus on each Una Merkle pimple which looks the same though our eyes have opened and shut—how many times since 1933?

What remains between this moment and my death? How will I grow old?—as though that question were not being answered every minute! Time for a few tears now: it has, after all been so long. While writing, the lamp shines across these icky ball-point smears transparent as infant wrists, and this transparency *in itself* saddens me—inexplicable as menopause depression. Did *high* and *low* musically to old Greeks mean any more to them on our terms than current western male & female attitudes do to, say, Hindus? That sentence is unclear: Does high in music everywhere signify up? Is the man always on top? Can a man's wish for dominance exclude the brain? and does dominance necessarily mean top? (In choruses the woman is on top, the bass sustains. A ground bass—beneath, by definition—is the essence of maleness.) Could our perversions happily invert and intermesh? Will I cease courtesanship and become The Musician With Problems? If I died today it would not really be—well, *incorrect*. Now in the shadow of late thirties looking back I've obtained the best of that sought and produced of myself (through fever, shame, dignity): an artist and a person, not perhaps to other eyes, which see shreds, but to myself at least. To

announce that my advancement prefers the urgencies of pure
nature to urban ambitions would be to lie. Yet where and what
can I go and do that I've not gone and done better? Henceforth I
foresee only declining flesh inanely coupling with reason,
sputtering, a dimming of commitment, a pointless ending, a
silence which is not even a silence. Yet to kill myself now would
be less from not caring as from a certain wistfulness which, after
all, I suppose *is* caring. . . . Already I am becoming The
Musician With Problems, for many minutes have passed since I
wrote Time for a few tears now: yet the gift for self-dramatiza-
tion does not make nights less sleepless. Sleep isn't death.
Staying awake is.

Sexual intercourse: think of it, obsessing the heart, dominat-
ing logic, teasing nights, wasting whole days! Isn't it really—
well—rather silly, or at least senseless: two clumsy positions
rubbing like washboards with ugly grunts and an ultimate
thump that rhymes with nothing, except maybe "Go away!"—
when two minutes earlier, for some wild reason, it was almost "I
love you"? For that we walk the streets fifty-two weeks a year!

The horror of the carnal hunt, as though the cultural hunt
weren't sufficiently atrocious.

▼▼▼

*I am in love again for the first time. Need to giggle, to jump
up and down. Our planet, bulging with joy, seems too small,
etc.*

Did I write that! Are nearly two thousand days gone since the
fall of 1956 when I met Claude? How utterly remote, the
agonies of love when they're over, while those of work remain as
irksome (to put it mildly) as Damocles' sword! The comings and
goings, risings and fallings, the *breathings* of this diary appear,
with the overall scope of hindsight, more steady than a sleeper's.
Yet tonight, snared by details of other years, pausing at past
landmarks, I retrieve lost episodes with the identical instability
of their first occurrence.

These poor journals have never been those of a musician: musically I express myself elsewhere and otherwise. Today of course they have become (perhaps alas!) the jottings only of someone rapidly advancing, maybe decaying, who may feel a need for the fatal backward glance. But a glance at what? Because those things which are daily concerns are hardly discussed: family and close friends, compositions in progress, low points of the high life (as in the Paris diaries). Not even my state of mind, just a state of body. These journals then will provide only that backward glance toward a state of body denied or indulged. As to whether I had any life, or even lived, that may (or may not) be seen when I'm dead—if I die.

▼▼▼

If, after dying, I discover there's no Life After Death, will I be furious?

▼▼▼

Not to believe in love anymore means to believe in love. One must believe in the existence of something in order to disbelieve it.

▼▼▼

Weary of myself. So perhaps are my friends. So perhaps is nature, who will kill me off. But not all that soon—she doesn't love me enough. France will rejuvenate!

▼▼▼

If our year 1961 is the same upside-down and backward, and not until 6009 A.D. will the phenomenon recur, then we have five thousand and forty-eight years of waiting to sober up.

▼▼▼

Sitting in one denuded Manhattan room whose center contains a mountain of packing cases to be removed tomorrow by Robert Phelps. Without paying last month's rent I fly Friday for

London, meanwhile have already left, can only sit, wondering, in this denuded room for five days more.

Wondering about those three things (and there are only three) we all desire: success in love, success in society, success in our work. Any two of these may be achieved and possessed simultaneously, but not all three—there isn't time. If you think you have the three—beware! You're teetering on any abyss. You can't, with everyone's equalized happiness, have a lover *and* friends *and* career. And even just career and love, despite what they tell you, are, in the long run, mutually exclusive.

▼▼▼

Ignorance of the future is all that can save us. We need less the time to think than the time to think about what we think. Before finding the solution we must find the problem. Love, profession, society. Now I feel less than a flop in the first two. Assuming European doors will open as before, are love or acclaim also lurking? In my glib quick wit with smiles lighting, when others say: What! you sad? that's a laugh! Yet who ever shows his "real" side—assuming there is a real side? O God, when a whole life's spent wishing we could or had, then finding ourselves *in the fact* (as though suddenly) and wondering: well, this is it, and is this all? There must be something more! People keep wondering: where does the man leave off and the artist begin? This is where.